Philip Andrews-Speed, Xuanli Liao and Roland Dannreuther

The Strategic Implications of China's Energy Needs

Adelphi Paper 346

Oxford University Press, Great Clarendon Street, Oxford OX2 6DP
Oxford   New York
Athens Auckland Bangkok Bombay Calcutta Cape Town
Dar es Salaam Delhi Florence Hong Kong Istanbul Karachi
Kuala Lumpur Madras Madrid Melbourne Mexico City
Nairobi Paris Singapore Taipei Tokyo Toronto
and associated companies in
Berlin Ibadan

Oxford is a trade mark of Oxford University Press

Published in the United States
by Oxford University Press Inc., New York

First published July 2002 by **Oxford University Press** for
The International Institute for Strategic Studies
Arundel House, 13–15 Arundel Street, Temple Place, London WC2R 3DX
www.iiss.org

Director John Chipman
Editor Mats R. Berdal
Copy Editor Glen Quatermain

British Library Cataloguing in Publication Data
Data available

Library of Congress Cataloguing in Publication Data

ISBN 0-19-851675-4
ISSN 0567-932x

Contents

5   **List of Figures, Tables and Maps**

7   **Introduction**

11   Chapter 1   **China's Energy Security Policy**
  - *Energy Security 13*
  - *Why China has an Energy Security Problem 20*
  - *China's Energy Security Policy 24*
  - *Evaluation of China's Approach 42*

45   Chapter 2   **China's Energy Security Policymaking and Implementation**
  - *The Actors and Their Priorities 46*
  - *Xinjiang: The West-to-East Gas Pipeline 53*
  - *Central Asia: Gas from Turkmenistan and Oil from Kazakhstan 58*
  - *Russia: A Source of Oil and Gas 61*
  - *The Middle East: A Crucial Source of Oil 65*
  - *Conclusion 67*

71   Chapter 3   **The Strategic Implications of China's Energy Needs**
  - *Implications for Global Oil Supplies 74*
  - *Military and Security Implications 77*
  - *Geopolitical Implications for East Asia 82*
  - *Implications for Middle East Stability 89*
  - *Implications for Domestic Stability 93*

99   **Conclusion**

103 **Notes**

List of Figures, Tables and Maps

12 **Figure 1** Graph of supply and demand of commercial energy, 1980–2000

12 **Figure 2** Graph of oil supply and demand in China 1985–2000

14 **Table 1** A working classification of 'energy security' events, expanded and modified from that of Horsnell

16 **Table 2** Summary and classification of possible measures to enhance security of energy supply

21 **Table 3** Structure of primary energy consumption 1980–1999

23 **Table 4** Projections of total primary commercial energy demand in China to 2020

25 **Table 5** Projected oil demand in China to 2020

26 **Table 6** Projected gas demand in China to 2020

27 **Table 7** Estimates of China's reserves of oil, gas and coal

29 **Table 8** Projections of China's oil production to 2020

31 **Table 9** Projections of China's gas production to 2020

32 **Table 10** Projected levels of China's net oil imports to 2020

33 **Table 11** Forecast levels of gas imports

34 **Table 12** Main investments by Chinese petroleum companies in overseas oil and gas exploration and development

35 **Table 13** Share of global proven recoverable reserves of oil and gas in the 'belt' around China

37 **Map 1** Energy map of Asia-Pacific

38 **Figure 3** Changing share of sources for China's oil imports 1993–2000

39 **Figure 4** Exports and imports of crude oil and oil products from China 1990–2000

Introduction

China is to become increasingly dependent on imports of oil and gas. In the early 1990s China was a net exporter of oil; by 2020, it is probable that 60% of its oil and 30% of its natural gas will be imported. Ensuring that sufficient supplies of energy are provided at affordable prices, and without significant disruptions, is critical for China's economic development and prosperity. For the Chinese leadership, which has traditionally enjoyed a high degree of energy self-sufficiency, the challenge of ensuring a secure supply of imported energy is a new and increasingly significant factor in their foreign and security policy calculations. There is no longer the prospect of being a neutral and disinterested bystander to regional and global energy geopolitics. In a number of the most critical energy-rich regions, most notably in the Middle East, Russia and Central Asia, China now potentially has a direct economic interest in securing its energy requirements. Inevitably, external powers will have to adapt to the implications of China's changing energy needs and the prospect of a more dynamic and proactive Chinese presence in the global energy markets.

Developments in the late 1990s showed that China was not only thinking more seriously about its growing energy dependence but also acting more decisively. In particular, the state-owned oil company, China National Petroleum Company (CNPC), demonstrated its increasing confidence and its greater international engagement with major investments in overseas oil projects. In 1997, the decision by the CNPC to pledge $8 billion for oil concessions in Kazakhstan, Venezuela, Iraq and Sudan represented a significant change in strategic orientation and involved outbidding a number of major Western oil companies. In 1998, the first official visit of Jiang Zemin to Saudi Arabia highlighted the increased strategic importance of oil diplomacy in Chinese foreign policy. Jiang's celebration of the Sino-Saudi relationship as a 'strategic oil partnership' highlighted the geopolitical importance for Beijing of this diplomatic rapprochement. As in the Middle East, so in Russia and Central Asia, and even further away in Africa (Sudan) and Latin America (Venezuela), Chinese diplomacy has included a more substantive energy dimension which has provided a direct strategic rationale for its engagement. Closer to home, the resource dimension of border disputes, most notably in the South China Sea, and the fears of disruption of supplies along the sea lines of communication from the Middle East, have gained in strategic importance.

The principal objective of this Paper is to provide an in-depth analysis of China's energy security policy and to draw out and analyse the strategic implications of this policy, particularly as it potentially impacts on Western interests. There are three chapters in this Paper. The first chapter starts with an examination of the fundamental issues in energy security before moving on to provide an assessment of China's energy needs up to 2020, which includes projections for energy consumption, prospects for energy production and forecasts for levels of energy imports. This is followed by a critical assessment of the energy security policy that the Chinese government has pursued and the key decisions that have been made in implementing this policy. The main conclusion of this chapter is that, in comparison to the approaches taken by most Western states in their energy security policy, the Chinese government has adopted a more 'strategic' than 'market' approach to energy security. What is meant by this is that the government has placed most of its efforts on 'strategic' measures such as maximising domestic production of oil and gas, investing in overseas production, and enhancing political links with petroleum-exporting states. Considerably less progress has been made to promote more market-driven policies, such as the liberalisation of the internal energy markets and the introduction of measures to constrain demand in terms of transport policy. Only recently has the government announced the setting up of emergency response mechanisms.

The second chapter analyses the reasons why the Chinese government has decided to adopt this predominantly strategic approach. This involves an assessment of the Chinese policymaking process, identifying the key domestic actors in determining energy security policy and how they have contributed to policies and decisions. The analysis in this chapter provides the domestic policymaking context underlying and explaining the preference for 'strategic' rather than 'market-oriented' approaches to energy security. The chapter also demonstrates how China's growing import dependence has increasingly engaged the interest and involvement of the foreign and security policy community in Beijing. As such, energy security has moved from being a technical 'low politics' issue to a question of 'high politics'. Four case-studies are provided to illustrate how politico-security and strategic concerns have become entangled with the more strictly economic and efficiency considerations. These are the west-to-east gas pipeline from Xinjiang; energy projects in Central Asia; Sino-Russian energy linkages; and Chinese petroleum diplomacy in the Middle East.

The third and final chapter addresses the question of the implications, for the West, of China's energy security policy and its preference for a strategic rather than market-oriented approach to energy security. This involves a critical assessment of some of the most prominent fears and concerns of the Western strategic community; that China's import needs could lead to global energy scarcity; that China will use force, particularly in the South China Sea, to ensure security of supply; that it could lead Central Asia and Russia acquiescing to Chinese hegemony in exchange for guaranteed energy exports; or that China will be tempted to sell missile, nuclear and other destabilising technology in the Middle East in exchange for security of supply. The main conclusion of this chapter is that these fears, though legitimate, tend to be exaggerated and ignore the countervailing trends that suggest cooperation and integration are more probable outcomes of China's search for energy security than conflict and confrontation. Although such conflict and confrontation cannot be excluded, it is likely that, as an independent variable, energy security is unlikely to be the cause and that other considerations would be paramount, such as, for example, a severe deterioration in US-Sino relations.

Indeed, the main conclusion drawn from this Paper is that the main threat of China's current energy security policy is not primarily to its neighbours or other external powers but to its own domestic stability. This is because, if China fails to supplement its primarily strategically driven energy security policy with market-driven measures, the likely consequence would be to damage the prospects of economic growth, accentuate regional and social cleavages, and potentially undermine social and political stability. Taking these considerations into account, the West, and other interested external actors, have two ways in which they can help China in its quest for energy security. The first is to support the strategic measures that China has adopted in a manner which encourages regional cooperation and integration as against geopolitical competition and confrontation. The second is to provide advice and support for China to balance these strategic measures with the range of demand-side measures and market mechanisms which are vital both for a durable and long-term energy security policy and for the success of China's integration into the global economy.

Chapter 1

China's Energy Security Policy

Energy security has become an increasingly important concern to China's government since the mid-1990s as domestic energy production has failed to keep pace with demand (Fig. 1). This shortfall is not caused by an absolute shortage of primary energy resources because China has the third-largest reserves of coal in the world and is one of the top two consumers of coal. Rather, it arises from a shortage of energy in the forms required. A rapid growth in the use of road transport has driven a sustained rise in demand for oil products. Domestic production of oil has failed to keep pace, and so China became a net importer of oil in 1995 (Fig. 2). Demand for oil is set to grow indefinitely, while domestic production will soon reach a peak. By 2010 China will be one of the world's major oil importers. Consumption of gas will also rise through the government's determination to reduce the level of atmospheric pollution arising from the burning of coal. Though recent exploration campaigns have identified substantial new domestic gas reserves, the ambitious gasification plans will require China to slowly become a major importer of gas as well as oil. As a result, China's 30 years of energy self-sufficiency has drawn to a close and an era of growing dependence on overseas energy supplies has commenced.

This fundamental change of energy balance would have triggered a careful review of energy strategy in any country, let alone one such as China which prides itself on its self-sufficiency. Not surprisingly, security of energy supply, particularly of oil, has become an increasing concern for central government. This chapter

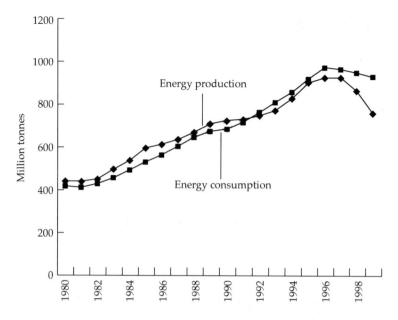

Figure 1 Graph of supply and demand of commercial energy, 1980–2000[16]

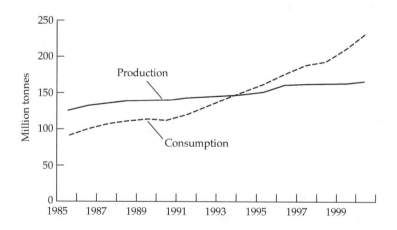

Figure 2 Graph of oil supply and demand in China 1985–2000[20]

first examines the issues lying behind the concept of energy security and the range of measures which may be taken to enhance a nation's security of energy supply. It then describes and evaluates the approach currently being taken by China.

Energy Security
What is Energy Security?

Energy security is commonly understood as 'the availability of energy at all times in various forms, in sufficient quantities, and at affordable prices'.[1] Either a rise in the price of energy or a disruption of energy supply may have a significant detrimental impact on an energy-importing country. Economic effects may include lower industrial output, a decline in investment, increased unemployment, reduced consumer demand, lower levels of welfare, inflation, a worsening balance of payments balance and an overall flow of resources from energy importing to energy exporting countries.[2] In the political sphere it has been argued that an energy-importing state may slip into a weak bargaining position with respect to the exporting states. It may lose flexibility in the formulation of foreign policy, and ultimately could suffer a reduced military capability. In a regional context, conflict between energy-importing countries may develop.[3] These considerations provide a valid reason for all countries to develop policies to enhance their security of energy supply. Markets alone cannot achieve a satisfactory level of security of supply in the long-term.

Threats to Energy Security

A number of different types of events may cause disruptions to energy supply or an increase in price. Two broad groups of event may be distinguished: events which are of global impact and those which impact a specific country or region (Table 1).

The global events are of concern to all oil and gas importing countries. The most common of these is the 'policy discontinuity' caused by OPEC policy decisions on output levels which are driven by a desire to raise or lower international crude oil prices. Such discontinuities are almost certain to occur every few years until better information on production and stock levels is available.[4] The impact of such a discontinuity is a relatively sudden and unpredictable change of oil prices. A long-term failure to invest in production, transportation or processing capacity could result in an absolute shortage of supply of energy with respect to the demand. This is the most serious energy security threat facing the world today. Such an event would have a serious impact on the econom-

Table 1 A working classification of 'energy security' events, expanded and modified from that of Horsnell[9]

Classification	Event
1. *Global events*	
a. Policy discontinuity	Reduction in output by producers, to raise prices
b. Fundamental discontinuity	Global shortage of production capacity
c. *Force majeure* disruption	Civil unrest, war, deliberate blockage of trade routes
d. Export disruption	Export cut-back by main exporters
e. Embargo disruption	Embargo by importers of a specific exporting state
2. *Local events*	
a. Embargo disruption	General embargo of specific importing state
b. Embargo disruption	Embargo of a specific importing state by a specific exporter or transit state
c. Logistical disruption	Accident, incident or terrorism, especially along transportation infrastructure
d. Local market disruption	By monopolist suppliers, by pressure groups, or through government mismanagement

ies of energy importing countries and on the global economy, and such impact could last a number of years while the necessary capacity is constructed.[5]

The remaining three events in the 'global' category (*force majeure*, export and embargo disruptions, Table 1) cover a variety of disruptions in or around the major oil and gas exporting states. Most of these types of event have their roots in political manoeuvres, either of importing states or of exporting states[6] and are unlikely to have a sustained detrimental impact on importers, for two reasons. Either the interests of the party causing the disruption are being damaged by the disruption, or alternative methods of trading and transport can be found.[7] In addition a limited number of states, such as Saudi Arabia, have surplus production capacity and could rapidly raise output in a crisis. Whether they would agree to do so is another matter. Only a major global or regional war could disrupt supplies for more than a few months.[8] What have been classified as 'local' events (Table 1) have the potential to cause much more damage to an importing country's energy supply. These local events fall into three categories: embargoes of various types, physical disruptions, and market disruptions.

A general embargo of a specific importing state, if effective, could bring a country to its knees very quickly. However, we believe that the probability is extremely low that such a policy would be agreed to by a large number of states and then that this blockade would be effectively implemented, especially in the case of a large country with a long coastline such as China. Again, such an event is only likely in a major regional or global war.

More probable is the deliberate disruption of an export flow by an exporting state or by a transit state. Such an action only has any meaning if applied to a pipeline rather than to shipping from a specific source. Ships can be diverted but pipelines are immovable. The exporting and transit states on a pipeline have some political leverage over the importing state and this can be used to disrupt flows in the short term in order to increase the exporting or transit country's bargaining power in some political or economic negotiation with one or more of the other states involved. A disruption of this type is likely to be short-lived because the interests of the disrupting state will also be affected by lost revenue, but such events may be frequent. In the future, China could be susceptible to such threats from Central Asian states and Russia, as well as from Mongolia if any import pipelines run across this country.

Accidents and, to a lesser extent, terrorism are endemic on some long-distance oil and gas transport routes, be they pipelines or sea lanes. Good management may reduce the frequency and impact of accidents. Likewise, persistent terrorist attacks on pipelines raise the cost of transport but need not greatly reduce the

Table 2 Summary and classification of possible measures to enhance security of energy supply, with an emphasis on oil.[13] Asterisks indicate extent to which particular measures have been taken in China. ***: Core component of current strategy. **: Substantial measures implemented. *: Relatively low priority to date

	'Strategic' approach	China's 'Strategic' measures	'Market' approach	China's 'Market' measures
Supply-side economic measures to reduce probability of disruption	• Control through state companies • Self reliance • Investment in domestic and overseas production and transportation	***	• Liberalise energy markets • Integrate with international markets • Encourage domestic and international investment in production and transportation	*

	Use administrative measures to:		Use market measures to:	
Demand-side economic measures to reduce probability of disruption	• Increase energy efficiency • Adjust transport policy • Diversify transport fuels	*	• Increase energy efficiency • Adjust transport policy • Diversify transport fuels	*
Political measures to reduce probability of disruption	• Enhance political links with energy exporters • Outward investment and aid to energy exporters	**	Promote the efficient functioning on international energy markets	*
Measures to reduce impact of disruption	• Strategic storage • Oil sharing • Emergency response procedures • Fuel switching • Surge capacity	*		

total flow provided the pipeline company can gain access to the pipeline. Petroleum pipelines from Central Asia are likely to be exposed to such threats, both within the Central Asian states and within far north-west China.

Events in the last two years have highlighted a new source of energy supply disruption in the developed countries, for example in California, but one which is not new to developing and transition economies – that is the disruption of local markets. Such disruptions may have many causes, such as pressure groups, government mismanagement, and monopolist behaviour. In China such threats could take the form of, for example, either the deliberate restriction of energy supply by a monopolist, or a badly designed or poorly implemented programme of liberalisation or privatisation.

From this brief survey we conclude that domestic and 'local' threats to energy supply may be just as important as those with a global origin. Indeed, in developing and transition countries the domestic threats may greatly outweigh the international ones. In the case of China, international events currently only pose a potential threat to oil supply. But, when gas imports commence, these supplies too will be at the mercy of external threats. Within China, the production and the transportation of all forms of energy are susceptible to a range of types of disruption.

Measures to Enhance Energy Security

A government of an energy-importing country may invest in a number of measures to enhance the country's security of energy supply. These may be categorised either as measures to reduce the probability of a supply disruption or as steps to minimise the impact of supply disruptions or price rises (Table 2). In simple terms, these measures may be characterised as reflecting a 'strategic' or 'market' approach to energy security. Long-term measures to reduce the probability of disruption may be either 'strategic' or 'market', but most measures to reduce the impact of a disruption are 'strategic' in nature.

The strategic approach would combine state-sponsored economic measures with political initiatives. Economic measures would include direct government participation in both enhancing domestic energy production and in investing in overseas sources of energy. Political links with energy exporters would be of great importance, and these would be supported by a range of economic measures such as aid, inward investment and sales of key goods. Governments pursuing this approach might not be overly concerned about the cost of implementation compared to the probability and impact of the disruptive event. The strategy of the Japanese government from the 1970s typifies this attitude[10] as does China's current approach.

The market approach would rely on the national and international energy markets and would seek to reduce the risk of disruption by improving the efficiency of these markets. The last 20 years have seen a tendency for the world's largest economies to prefer a market approach for long-term measures to energy security.[11] Thus recent reports on energy security issued by the US government, by the EC and by the Asia Pacific Energy Research Centre have emphasised the liberalisation of domestic energy markets, the promotion of investment in new capacity, and the improved flow of information.[12]

Two phenomena underpin this increasing trust in and reliance on market measures since the oil crises of the 1970s. The first is the development of regional and global energy markets. In the case of oil and coal truly global markets have emerged, though the amount of coal traded internationally is relatively small. Both gas and electricity are now being traded internationally across regional markets. This has been made possible through the construction of long-distance transportation networks and by deliberate efforts to reduce barriers to investment and trade. The coming years will see an increased trend to truly international and spot trade of LNG (liquefied natural gas) and the gradual demise of the long-term contract. The second change has been the rapid lowering of barriers to investment in the international energy sector. Few countries are now closed to foreign investment in oil and gas production, and many governments are taking steps to permit investment in their domestic gas and electricity supply industries.

Despite this increasing globalisation of energy markets, the fact that some 60% of the world's oil reserves and 30% of gas reserves are located in the Middle East necessarily results in all governments placing considerable emphasis on selected strategic measures to strengthen their security of energy supply. Since the events of 11 September 2001, many governments have been re-evaluating the implications of dependence on these oil supplies. The continued importance of OPEC in determining the direction of oil price changes adds an unpredictable political element to oil markets. That being the case, most players in the international oil markets prefer predictability to volatility, whether they are OPEC or non-OPEC producing governments, state or private companies, or consumer governments.

Whether their supply-side focus is strategic or market driven, most governments also consider demand-side mechanisms to reduce vulnerability to supply disruptions. These may include enhancing energy efficiency, seeking substitutes for oil, and promoting public transport (Table 2). The mechanisms used to implement these measures will to a great extent depend on the nature of the domestic energy markets. Market mechanisms may be appropriate in a liberalised energy market, but a regulatory approach will be needed where the energy sector remains controlled as is the case in China.

These long-term strategies, whether based on markets or on strategic mechanisms, should be supplemented by measures to address the short-term impact of an actual supply disruption or a price spike. The key steps are to establish emergency storage and to draw up an emergency response plan. Implementation takes time, money and careful consideration of a number of issues.[14]

A final consideration in energy security is the transportation of energy. Energy has no value unless it is available at the point of use. Of special concern are those forms of energy, which rely on fixed transport networks, such as gas and electricity. In most countries the government will be involved in the planning and possibly the actual construction of these networks.

Why China has an Energy Security Problem
China's Recent Energy Supply and Demand

China's economic growth and industrialisation has required a prodigious increase in energy supply. Since 1980 the annual consumption of commercial energy[15] has risen by approximately 250%

Table 3 Structure of primary energy consumption 1980–1999[17]

	1980	1985	1990	1995	1999
Coal	72.3%	75.9%	76.1%	74.7%	70.6%
Oil	20.9%	17.0%	16.6%	17.4%	20.7%
Natural gas	2.8%	2.2%	2.1%	1.8%	2.3%
Primary electricity	4.0%	4.9%	5.2%	6.0%	6.4%

(Fig. 1). This rise in demand for energy provided the government with a major challenge. It responded by introducing measures to raise the output of coal, the most readily accessible form of primary energy in the country. China has the world's third largest reserves of coal and has been the largest producer of coal since 1991 when it overtook the US. From 1980 to 1990 the contribution of coal to China's energy sector rose from 72% to 76% before falling sharply in the late 1980s (Table 3). At the same time the government invested heavily in hydro-electricity and, to a lesser extent, in nuclear power. The output of crude oil and natural gas also rose, but their relative share of energy consumption declined. The balance between the supply and demand for primary energy stayed roughly in balance until the mid-1990s.

The ability of China to provide for most of its own energy requirements from domestic sources has depended as much on increasing the efficiency of energy use as on producing more energy. Though still high by the standards of developing countries, China's energy intensity has declined substantially during the last 20 years. Two factors have contributed to this reduction of energy intensity. First, the structure of the economy has changed. The role of the service sector has grown, while the balance between heavy and light industry is generally shifting towards light industry. Second, the government has introduced a wide range of measures to increase the efficiency of energy end-use.[18]

In the middle and late 1990s, two dramatic changes took place in the balance of energy supply and demand. The first change occurred in 1995 when China's consumption of oil exceeded its domestic production for the first time (Fig. 2). From being one of the world's major net exporters of oil, China was now a net importer, and the level of net imports has steadily increased since then. This situation has been caused by a substantial rise in demand for oil products, mainly for transportation, combined with a failure to raise significantly the level of domestic oil production.

The second hiatus occurred in 1998 and 1999 when energy consumption in China fell for two successive years (Fig. 1). At the same time, stocks of coal had built up to record levels as a result of years of over-production. In 1998 the Chinese government embarked on a programme to cut back on coal production which has been sustained through at least 2001. This fall in energy demand is best explained by a combination of general economic slowdown related to the Asian crisis, a decline in output from energy-intensive industries, closures of inefficient state factories and a general increase of end-use efficiency,[19] as well as some substitution of coal by gas. At the same time the demand for oil and electricity flattened temporarily before picking up again in 2000.

China is not alone in having a high rate of increase of demand for energy and especially for oil. The average annual rise of oil consumption for the whole Asia-Pacific region has been running at about 3–5% for most of the last 15 years, compared to 1% or less for North America and Europe combined. Thus the Asia-Pacific region now accounts for some 27% of the world's annual consumption of oil compared to 17% in 1980.

China's Future Energy Demand

Any projection of future total energy demand in China depends on a number of factors such as the rate of economic growth, the structure of the economy and the level of end-use energy efficiency, each of which is difficult to forecast. This difficulty is enhanced in China by the government's ability to dramatically and suddenly change policy, and thus influence energy consumption to a greater degree than is possible in a market economy. Most projections envisage that China's primary energy consumption increases by at least 200% during the 20 years to 2020 (Table 4). The critical strategic issue, for both energy policy and implications for foreign policy, is the future energy mix rather than the absolute

Table 4 Projections of total primary commercial energy demand in China to 2020, in millions of tonnes of oil equivalent[21]

	2000	2005	2010	2015	2020
BP, 2001	768				
Medlock and Soligo, 1999			1405–1773	1575–2189	1761–2691
IEA, 2000			1426		1937
Jia et al., 1999			1496–1587		
Zhou and Zhou, 1999		1180	1350	1550	1770

level of energy consumption. Recent trends and analyses suggest that the coming 20 years will see a rise in the proportion of oil and gas consumption at the expense of coal.[22]

The need for oil products for road transport is the single most important factor driving China's increasing demand for oil, and this will continue to be the case in the short-term – say ten to 15 years. Beyond this, the demand for oil will depend on a number of inter-related factors:

- The rate of economic growth in China: higher growth will result in higher demand.
- China's transport policy: in recent years the government has appeared to actively encourage private car use, has kept petrol prices low and has invested relatively little in urban public transport systems. A change of emphasis could substantially reduce the rate of increase of demand for oil.
- The development and application of new technologies to the transport sector, such as coal-to-liquids or fuel cells.

Given that a high degree of uncertainty exists for each of these variables, it is hardly surprising that forecasts for China's oil demand over the next 20 years show considerable variation (Table 5). A consensus seems to exist that annual demand is likely to rise from a present level of around 230 million tonnes to 300 million tonnes by 2010 and at least 400 million tonnes by 2020, though unexpectedly low rates of economic growth would reduce demand to below these levels. Over this period China's share of world oil consumption will probably rise from its current level of about 6% to as high as 8–10%. [23]

Since the mid-1990s the Chinese government has placed great emphasis on developing a domestic gas market. Before this time, prices for gas were so low that they provided no incentive for the state companies to explore and develop gas deposits. As a result, gas has consistently accounted for only about 2% of the primary energy consumption (Table 3). The priority for future gas use in most of China will be to substitute for coal in electrical power generation and residential use. Any forecasts of future gas consumption have to be closely tied to the availability of developed reserves, either domestic or overseas, and of transport infrastructure, either pipelines or LNG. In addition, distribution infrastructure and gas-consuming appliances must be in place. Thus all current forecasts of gas consumption are based on certain assumptions concerning the rate of development of these reserves and the rate of development of infrastructure.

Both Chinese and Western forecasts of annual demand for gas in China show a substantial rise from current levels just above 20 billion cubic metres to 75–100 billion cubic metres by 2010 and 100–200 billion cubic metres by 2020 (Table 6).

The share of hydro-electricity in China's power generation is set to rise during the coming years, especially when the Three-Gorges Dam is commissioned in the year 2009. During the following years it is hoped that hydro-electricity will account for up to 20–22% of power generation, up from 18% in the 1990s. [25] Nuclear power continues to play a small but growing part in China's electricity sector.

Coal will continue to dominate China's primary energy consumption, but it will progressively be substituted by gas and hydro-electricity. By the year 2020 coal is likely to account for about 60% of China's primary energy consumption. [26]

China's Energy Security Policy

China's priority since the mid-1990s has been to address the economic and political costs and risks to the country of increasing

Table 5 Projected oil demand in China to 2020, in millions of tonnes[24]

	2000	2005	2010	2015	2020
BP, 2001	227				
Medlock and Soligo, 1999			269–349	303–437	340–544
IEA, 2000			371		541
Downs, 2000					440
Cordesman, 1998		280	350	394	575
Jia *et al.*, 1999			210		
APERC, 2000		259–277		314–341	
Shi et al., 1999			265		330
Gao, 2000			275–298	325–355	
Wang, 2000		238		325	
Zhou and Zhou, 1999		250	300	350	400

long-term dependence on overseas sources of oil and gas. The four main policy objectives have been: to maximise domestic output of oil and gas; to diversify the sources of oil purchased through the international markets; to invest in overseas oil and gas resources through the Chinese national petroleum companies, focusing on Asia and the Middle East; and to construct the infrastructure to bring this oil and gas to market.[28]

The underlying philosophy appears to be that China cannot afford to be heavily dependent on international markets for oil and therefore the government must direct the flow of investment into projects which reduce this dependence. A second consideration underlying this approach has been the military and strategic concern that China is vulnerable to a blockade of sea-lanes either in the Malacca Straits or in the South and East China Seas. Domestic energy resources and pipelines from adjacent Asian countries would substantially reduce this risk.[29] Little sustained

Table 6 Projected gas demand in China to 2020, in billions of cubic metres[27]

	2000	2005	2010	2015	2020
BP, 2001	27.3				
IEA, 2000			62		123
Fesharaki *et al.*, 1998			78		154
Downs, 2000					154–266
Cordesman, 1998		67	84	92	103
Xu, 1999			>76		>115
ERI, 1999			96		204
Paik, 1999			95		140
Zhang and Wang, 1998		65	121	160	193
Gao, 2000			75–90	150–200	
Zhou and Zhou, 1999		52	100	150	200
Jia *et al.*, 2000			95–120		147–245

progress has been made on implementing other proposals to enhance China's security of oil supply: constraining the demand for oil; deregulating the internal oil markets; and putting in place emergency response measures.

In the case of gas, the government's approach has been to direct short-term efforts into developing a substantial domestic gas industry fed by domestic gas resources. In the longer-term, gas imports will be supplied by pipeline from Russia, and to a lesser extent as LNG to coastal provinces.

Exploiting Domestic Resources

The drive to maximise the exploitation of domestic energy resources comes naturally to a China which has emphasised

Table 7 Estimates of China's reserves of oil, gas and coal. mmt = million tonnes; tcm = trillion cubic metres[33]

	Quantity	Source
Oil Proven recoverable	3,300 mmt	BP, 2001
Possible ultimate recoverable	13,000–15,000 mmt	Zhu and Song, 2000
Gas Proven recoverable	1.3 tcm 1.37 tcm 1.51 tcm	USEIA, 2000 BP, 2001 Zhou, 1999
Possible ultimate recoverable	11.5 tcm 7–10 tcm 11 tcm	Zhou, 1999 Zhu and Song, 2000 Xu, 1999
Coal Proven recoverable	114,000 mmt	BP, 2001

self-reliance since the Communist Party took over the government in 1949. The state petroleum companies have been pressurised for several years to find and develop new oil resources, especially in the west, and to maintain production levels in the east. Enormous quantities of money have been spent onshore by Chinese state companies and offshore by Chinese and foreign investors for relatively modest reward.

China's proven recoverable reserves of oil and gas (Table 7) are modest by international standards, amounting to just 2% and 1% of globally proven recoverable reserves respectively. However, this apparent similarity between oil and gas masks a fundamental difference. Most of the oil-bearing basins in China are well explored and the largest oil fields have been producing for 30 years or more, whereas systematic exploration for natural gas in China only started in the mid-1990s.

The failure to substantially raise the output of crude oil in the 1980s and early 1990s was one of the great disappointments in

China's energy sector. Offshore exploration has led to a steady series of modest discoveries over the last 20 years, yet these fields still account for less than 10% of the country's oil output. The disputed territories of the East China Sea and of the South China Sea have been touted as holding great promise. Little geological evidence exists to support this view.

The policy to accelerate development in the west resulted in a short-lived increase of output in the mid-1990s just when China had become a net importer of oil. But this increase has proven unsustainable and oil production has now, to all intents and purposes, flattened (Fig. 2).

Projections for oil production levels in the year 2010 vary from 155 million to 195 million tonnes per year (Table 8). By 2020 production may have fallen below the level of 2010 unless major new discoveries are made. However, such pessimistic forecasts may yet be invalidated by the unpredictable technological advances which permit additional recovery from existing fields, the development of fields previously viewed as uneconomic, or the discovery of new accumulations.

China's domestic supply of crude oil does not come cheaply. Production costs are estimated to vary from US$5–6 per barrel in the mature fields of north-east China, to US$10 per barrel in the Tarim Basin, to as high as US$13 per barrel in other basins.[30] These figures may also be referred to as 'lifting costs' and exclude exploration, development and transport costs. China's average onshore lifting costs are about US$12 per barrel, 50% more than the world average[31] and considerably more than those in the Middle East which are nearer US$2–3 per barrel. Offshore fields contribute more than 6% of China's domestic supply of oil and are much more modern and better managed than the onshore fields. Even so the production costs are reported to be US$10 per barrel.[32]

The domestic oil refining industry almost doubled in capacity from 145 million tonnes per year in 1990 to 270 million tonnes per year in 2000. At the same time the throughput rose from 110 million tonnes per year to only 210 million tonnes per year.[35] The large difference between the current capacity and the utilisation reflects a combination of technical inefficiencies, a mismatch between the technical specifications of the refineries and the

Table 8 Projections of China's oil production to 2020, in millions of tonnes[34]

	2000	2005	2010	2015	2020
BP, 2001	162				
IEA, 2000					130
Medlock and Soligo, 1999		155	155		
Downs, 2000					180
Cordesman, 1998		175	180	180	175
APERC, 2000			195		
Jia *et al.*, 1999		161–174	170–188		
Shi *et al.*, 1999			180		200
Gao, 2000			185–195	200–210	
Wang, 2000		178–188		205–225	
Zhou and Zhou, 1999		165	170	175	180

specific oil products required by the market, and inflated figures for refining capacity. Some of the unused capacity is in the form of small refineries which are inefficient and polluting, and which have been the target of a recent programme of closure. A further factor which restricts the total refinery throughput is the inability of much of the capacity to cope with the sour crude oils[36] from the Middle East. China's refinery industry was built to take the oil from Chinese oil fields which is not sour. The import of similar oil from Indonesia and Oman was possible, but the sour crudes from the major Gulf exporters requires refineries to be built from higher-grade steel. A programme of refinery upgrading is in progress. Only about 30 million tonnes, or 10%, of China's refinery capacity could take sour crude in the year 2000 but this is set to rise to 56 million tonnes by 2005.

Natural gas, in contrast to oil, has not been the subject of major exploration campaigns until the late 1990s. There is considerable room for optimism that substantial new reserves will be discovered and that the ultimate level of recoverable reserves could be eight to ten times what is proven today. Thus the forecasts of China's domestic production of natural gas show a considerable jump from 27 billion cubic metres in 2000 to 60–75 billion cubic metres by 2010 and more than 100 billion cubic metres in 2020 (Table 9). The major constraints are a potential shortage of capital and the lack of a coherent national gas policy.[37] Most of China's gas reserves are far from the markets, and therefore billions of dollars are required for pipeline construction. The government has re-voked the ban on foreign ownership of pipelines and has invited foreign companies to participate in the construction and operation of gas domestic pipelines.

These reserves and forecasts for natural gas omit one poten-tially important source of supply, which is coal-bed methane. With its enormous coal resources there is a good chance that China will be able to commercially exploit significant quantities of methane trapped within the coal fields. Tests have been going on for nearly ten years, but it is not yet possible to confidently predict the level of reserves and possible production rates. If the optimistic esti-mates are proven correct then coal-bed methane could provide a substantial boost to China's drive for clean energy (Table 9).

For coal and hydro-electricity production, the government's objectives are quite clear. Since 1998 the government has suc-ceeded in substantially reducing the national output of coal to below 1000 million tonnes, down from nearly 1400 million tonnes in 1996, as well as reducing the level of stocks, which had built up to nearly 200 million tonnes in previous years. The twin challenges are to keep the level of production low by controlling output from small mines at the same time as investing in new large mines to secure the output of coal in the long-term. At the same time, the government has invested billions of dollars in large hydro-electric power schemes such as the Three Gorges and Ertan which will contribute a significant proportion of the electrical power supply of central and eastern regions of China.

The Growth of Energy Imports

Forecasting the level of imports for any form of primary energy involves the integration of two parameters, supply and demand,

Table 9 Projections of China's gas production to 2020, both conventional natural gas and coal-bed methane, in billions of cubic metres per year[38]

Gas	2000	2005	2010	2015	2020
Natural gas					
BP, 2001	27.7				
Xu, 1999			62–73		100–127
IEA, 2000					120
Fesharaki *et al.*, 1998				80–100	
Downs, 2000					106
ERI, 1999			70–75		100–150
Paik, 1999			72		95
Zhang and Wang, 1998		35	71	81	93
Jia *et al.*, 2000			54–73		92–110
Zhou and Zhou, 1999		40	70	85	100
Coal-bed methane					
Zhang and Wang, 1999		10	20	30	40
China internet source		3–4	10	20	

which themselves are fraught with uncertainty. Added to which is the ability of the Chinese government to vary the level of imports and exports and yet keep the level of net imports the same.

A number of forecasts of net oil imports in the year 2010 made by non-Chinese specialists lie close to 150 million tonnes (Table 10), which is similar to the predicted level of crude oil production in China at that time. Thus China would be importing some 50% of its oil requirements, compared to 30% in 2000. Chinese estimates of net imports are substantially lower. The main

Table 10 Projected levels of China's net oil imports to 2020, in millions of tonnes per year[39]

	2000	2005	2010	2015	2020
BP, 2001	70				
CSIS, 1999		80	150		
APCSS, 1999			150		
Fesharaki *et al.*, 1998		100	155		275
Medlock and Soligo, 1999			100–200		
Downs, 2000					260
Cordesman, 1998					250
IEA, 2000			230		411
Jia *et al.*, 1999			16–46		
Shi *et al.*, 1999			75–85		130
APERC, 2000			146		
Gao, 2000			90–103	125–145	
Wang, 2000		50–60		100–120	
Zhou and Zhou, 1999		85	130	175	220

uncertainty with respect to net oil imports is the level of demand, given that most analysts are confident that China's oil production has nearly reached a peak. The absolute quantity of oil imports would almost certainly continue to increase during the following decade and could exceed 250 million tonnes by 2020. This would place China on a par as an oil importer with Japan today.

The level of future natural gas imports to China will be critically dependent on the rate at which the infrastructure for imports is constructed, whether that is in the form of pipelines or LNG terminals. This in turn depends on a number of domestic political and international political factors which will be discussed

Table 11 Forecast levels of gas imports in billion cubic metres per year[41]

	2005	2010	2015	2020
Paik, 1999		23		45
Zhou, 1999		21–26		54–104
Zhang and Wang, 1998	20	30	50	60

in the following chapters, as well as on the availability of finance. The forecasts in Table 11 would be consistent with one major import pipeline project being operational by 2010 and a second by 2020. The LNG project currently under construction in Guangdong has a planned capacity of 6.5 billion cubic metres by 2010.

China has consistently been a net exporter of coal. It exports coal to neighbouring countries in north-east Asia and the proportion of these exports rose from 1–2% of total coal output during the 1980s and 1990s. The sudden downturn in domestic coal demand in 1998 triggered an export drive so that by 2001 some 8% of China's coal, 86 million tonnes, was exported. The level of coal imports to coastal China has remained consistent at about 2 million–3 million tonnes per year, though may rise as the demand for steam coal and semi-anthracite grows.[40]

No significant trade in electricity to and from China exists at present, though the Energy Working Group of the Asia-Pacific Economic Cooperation (APEC) is currently evaluating a number of potential international power grids. Two of these involve China, and would connect the country with Russia and with Korea and Japan respectively. In the short-term such inter-connections do not seem necessary, as China's power supply problems can be largely addressed through the commissioning of new hydro-electric schemes and by enhancing the domestic transmission and distribution systems.

Investment in Overseas Energy Resources
Since the mid-1990s official and academic documents in China

Table 12 Main investments by Chinese petroleum companies in overseas oil and gas exploration and development; this does not include service or construction contracts in the oil and gas industry, or investment in other sectors[47]

Country	Project name or location	Project nature	Approx. date	Value US$m
Kazakhstan	Aktyubinsk	Oil development & production	1997	4,000
Kazakhstan	Uzen	Oil development & production	1997	1,300
Kazakhstan	JV with ONGC of India	Oil exploration	1998	
Turkmenistan		Oil field services	1997 & 2002	14 & 52
Azerbaijan	Kyursangi, Karabagly	Oil field development	2002	52
Russia	East Siberia	Oil exploration & production	2001	
Iran	Balal	Gas/Oil development & production	1999	
Iraq	Al Ahdab	Oil development & production	1996/7	1,300
Kuwait	Various	Oil development & production, and refineries		3,000
Sudan	Various fields	Oil development & production, & pipeline	1998	700
Venezuela	Two fields	Exploration	1998	385
Peru	Talara	Oil field rehabilitation	1993	25
Mongolia		Oil production & refining	1998	30
Indonesia	Repsol's assets	Exploration & production	2002	585
Papua New Guinea	Block 160 and Kamusi	Exploration	1994	
Egypt		Oil and gas development	1999	
Thailand	Banya	Oil development & production	1993	
Canada	Calgary	Oil production	1992/3	11
Nigeria	Niger delta	Exploration	1998	
Nigeria	Chad Basin	Oil exploration	1997	

Table 13 Share of global proven recoverable reserves of oil and gas in the 'belt' around China[43]

Country/Region	Oil %	Gas %
Russia	4.6	32
Central Asia	1.7	5
Gulf	65	35
China	2.3	0.9

have proclaimed the virtues of China's petroleum companies investing in overseas oil exploration and production in order to secure supplies of 'Chinese' crude oil, which could then be refined in China.[42] The first projects in the early 1990s were generally far from China and had the character of experiments. Only in the late 1990s did sizeable commitments start to be made, the largest of which were in Kazakhstan and Sudan (Table 12).

At the heart of this strategy lies the recognition that China is surrounded by a 'belt' of untapped oil and gas reserves in Russia, Central Asia and the Middle East (Table 13). In all three regions, considerable potential exists for further discoveries, especially in Central Asia and eastern Russia, which are relatively lightly explored.

With the exception of the petroleum resources in the Middle East, all of this oil and gas production could be delivered to consumers in central and eastern China via pipeline. For this reason Chinese investment activity has been focused on Central Asia and Russia. Oil from the Middle East and other remote regions could be shipped directly to China along a supply chain, which could be under Chinese management from start to finish. Together, these pipelines and shipping routes would, supposedly, substantially reduce China's exposure to disruption in the international markets and to military blockade. A specific target had been set for the oil industry to secure supplies of 50 million tonnes per year from overseas production by 2010 [44], but this plan was greatly dependent on the construction of an oil pipeline from Kazakhstan to China. If, as it seems, plans for this pipeline have been shelved indefinitely, then this target for 'Chinese' oil from overseas may not be reached.

A lull in China's overseas oil and acquisitions at the end of the 1990s came to an abrupt end in late 2001 and early 2002. CNOOC purchased all the Indonesian assets of Spain's Repsol-YPF for US $585 million and, in Azerbaijan, CNPC bought a share of two oil fields for US $52 million. At the same time CNPC has been examining investment opportunities in east Siberia. These activities would appear to indicate that the overseas investment strategy held by both the Chinese government and the petroleum companies is still being pursued, and that its implementation has been aided by the profits earned by the companies during the period of high oil prices at the turn of the century. Energy security fears after 11 September may have accelerated the conclusion of some of these deals.

Energy Transportation Infrastructure

Sufficient and effective transportation infrastructure is essential for all forms of energy if that energy is to be used efficiently. For China, gas pipelines are a crucial element of its current energy strategy and a regional approach is necessary.[45] The main sources of gas supply lie either in the north and west of the country, far from potential markets in the east, or in Russia. Six new domestic gas pipelines have been proposed to transport gas from new and existing fields in the north, north-west and south-west of the country. The longest of these will bring gas from the Tarim basin to Shanghai (See Map 1). In addition, a number of other import pipelines have been proposed, from the Irkutsk and Yakutia regions of eastern Siberia, from Sakhalin in the Russian Far East, from western Siberia, from Turkmenistan and even from Southeast Asia. None of these import pipelines have received official approval from the Chinese government, and no order of priority has been announced, for two reasons: first, the focus has switched to constructing the domestic pipeline from north-west China; and, second, the Chinese government appears to be having difficulty

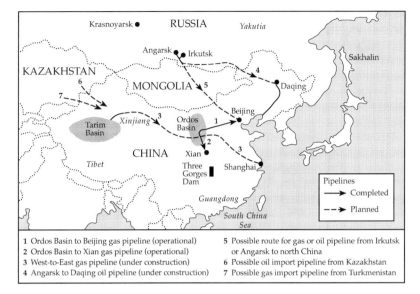

Map 1 Energy map of Asia-Pacific

determining which project satisfies its strategic goals most completely. In the meantime the first LNG import project in China is now underway in Guangdong Province in the south-east of the country.

A number of oil import routes from Russia are also at various stages of planning. The first is a crude oil pipeline from the Angarsk region of Siberia, which is close to the gas fields of Irkutsk. This pipeline could be completed by 2005 and it is planned to transport up to 20 million tonnes per year of Russian crude oil to north-east China.[46] This plan seems to have superseded an idea to pipe the crude oil to ports in the Russian Far East for onward shipment to China. At the same time, new discoveries in the Krasnoyarsk region of Siberia are prompting suggestions that oil from there could also be exported to China.

Russia is also being considered by CNPC as a buyer of crude oil to be produced from its fields in Kazakhstan. Under a swaps arrangement Russian crude would then be shipped to China from ports on the Pacific coast. Plans for a crude oil pipeline from Kazakhstan to central and eastern China, which had appeared to have been shelved because of the high cost, may be resurrected. The events of 11 September have prompted a re-evaluation by the

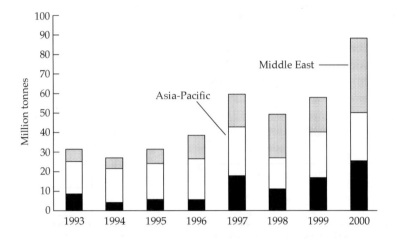

Figure 3 Changing share of sources for China's oil imports 1993–2000 (Asia-Pacific, Middle East, and others)[50]

Chinese government of the implications of their increasing dependence on the Middle East for supplies of oil. A pipeline from Kazakhstan may be an attractive, though expensive, security measure.

As part of the strategy to enhance the effectiveness of the energy sector, the Chinese government has for several years been spending substantial sums of money on upgrading and expanding the domestic transportation networks for coal and electrical power. A key objective is to have a completely inter-connected national power grid by the year 2010.[48]

Supplies from the International Markets

However much China invests in domestic and overseas oil and gas production, it is likely to continue to be heavily dependent on international oil markets and regional or global gas markets. The government has pursued four strategic goals with respect to oil imports: it has diversified the source of these imports; it has raised the proportion of crude oil to oil products in these imports, thus sustaining and enhancing China's refining industry; it continues to bring the domestic pricing mechanism for crude oil and oil products more in line with international markets; and it continues to conclude long-term sales arrangements and build political ties with key suppliers rather than rely on the spot markets.

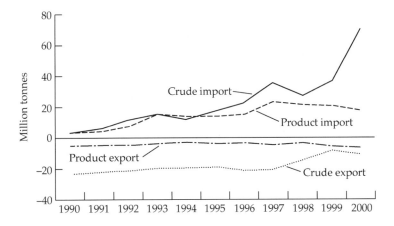

Figure 4 Exports and imports of crude oil and oil products from China 1990–2000[51]

The 1990s saw China make a strategic shift in its sources of oil imports. In the early 1990s more than half of this trade came from the Asia-Pacific region, mainly Indonesia and Malaysia. As China became a net importer of oil, it deliberately sought to raise the proportion of imports from the Middle East and other regions such as Africa and Latin America (Fig. 3). However, its ability to take Middle Eastern crude oil was constrained by the need to upgrade its refineries to take the sour crude which typifies the Gulf. Since 1997, China has established long-term supply arrangements with Gulf states such as Saudi Arabia, Iran, Oman and Yemen. This provides both sides with a sense of security – for supplies in the case of China and sales in the case of the Gulf states. At the same time, the Gulf states have been actively pressing the Chinese government to allow them to construct refineries in China. Thus it is reasonable to assume that an increasing share of China's oil imports will be in the form of crude oil from the Gulf.

Two features of oil imports, which China can control, are the actual quantity of imports and the forms of these imports. Figure 4 shows how the level of imports and exports of both crude oil and oil products varied during the 1990s. During the early 1990s imports of crude oil and oil products rose in parallel until 1995 when the government made a deliberate policy-decision to take most imports in the form of crude oil in order to make the best use of China's existing refinery capacity and related labour force.[49] The second point to emerge from Figure 4 is that China maintained the level of exports until 1998 when low international prices led the government to cut back on exports of crude oil to Japan.

To date, China has imported no natural gas. The first import project to be commissioned will be the LNG terminal in Guangdong. As of the middle of 2001, the source of supply for this project had not been decided, but a number of potential suppliers exist in both the Middle East and Asia-Pacific. It is likely that the first gas import pipeline to China will be from one of the several Russian gas fields under discussion, whether or not Chinese companies hold a stake in that field. Subsequent pipelines might also be from Russia.

Constraining Demand

The Chinese government has taken few steps to constrain the growth of demand for oil, despite recommendations to do so through conservation, efficiency and substitution.

Political pressures and relatively high international oil prices have constrained the government's plans to impose higher taxes on transport fuels and thus consumer prices for gasoline and diesel are arguably too low to encourage savings or the use of more fuel-efficient vehicles.[52] Steps have been taken in some cities to promote the use of gas in public road transport. The efficacy of such measures is presently constrained by a shortage of gas supply in most cities, and by the small number of buses compared to the number of private vehicles. This is connected to a lack of a coherent policy for urban and suburban transport in most Chinese cities. Over the past 20 years, very little investment has been directed at subway systems or in suburban rail networks.

Proposals to derive transport fuels from coal or gas[53] are constrained from being implemented on a large scale by the cost: the high cost of the coal liquefaction process; the high cost of China's gas for use in gas-to-oil technology; and the high cost of the infrastructure for private gas-fuelled vehicles.

Demand for natural gas can be constrained by infrastructure and price. If the infrastructure is not in place, gas cannot be consumed. At present China's challenge is to get the gas to the consumer. New gas supply is being charged to consumers at levels which should provide for costs to be recovered and which are sufficiently high to encourage economic use.

Emergency Response

China appears not to have put in place contingency measures to cope with a sudden disruption of oil supplies, despite calls to do so.[54] The state oil companies have substantial storage capacity for oil, though reliable numbers are difficult to find.[55] However, these have not been treated as a national strategic reserve. In June 2001 the government announced plans to develop a strategic oil reserve of 6 million tonnes by 2005 and 15 million tonnes by 2010.[56] These reserves are to be held by both the government and the companies, but they will be under government management. These quantities amount to barely more than one month of projected net oil imports and fall far short of earlier proposals to build the reserve at almost twice this rate.[57] This emergency storage may be supplemented by surge production capacity.

Gas storage plays an important role in managing the seasonal fluctuations in demand for gas, and may also be used as a strategic reserve. Though the pipeline from the Ordos Basin in north China to Beijing was completed in 1997, only in 2000 did construction start on storage.[58] It does not appear that this storage is intended to cover unexpected disruptions to supply.

Market Measures

The importance of deregulating China's energy companies and liberalising energy markets, trade and prices has been highlighted by foreign commentators but has been recognised by only a few Chinese.[59]

In 1998, the Chinese government carried out a major restructuring of the government and of state companies in the energy sector, and set up a mechanism to ensure that domestic oil prices more closely reflected international market prices.[60] However, these measures resulted in little genuine liberalisation of the domestic energy sector. Most energy production, transportation and supply are controlled by companies owned by the state at different levels of government. Energy prices are still set or constrained by government agencies, as are import and export quotas. Little genuine competition exists, except possibly in the retail of oil products. Most aspects of the internal energy market are highly controlled and there is little integration with international markets.

Radical reform of the state energy enterprises and energy markets is constrained by a range of political, structural, and technical factors,[61] and the Chinese government is well-advised not to rush into any hurried programme of reform. That being the case, the apparent lack of a coherent long-term strategy for the development of the energy sector does not bode well for the country's security of energy supply.

If and how China reforms its energy sector may have significant influence on the nature of its energy security policy and on the likely success and cost of this policy. Should China fail to embark on a systematic and far-reaching programme of reform and liberalisation, the state companies will remain very powerful, integration with international energy markets will be restrained, and approaches to energy security will continue to be strategic in nature. Though security of supply may indeed be enhanced, the cost to the country will be great. The main supply risks will be domestic and will take the form of inadequate or inappropriate investment, or abuse of power by monopoly suppliers.

If China formulates a strategy for energy reform and liberalisation, and if it begins to implement it in a systematic manner, then the whole approach to energy security can become more market-oriented. Along with adherence to WTO requirements, these reforms would allow China to become progressively more integrated with international energy markets, and to enhance its security of supply at relatively little cost. On the other hand, should the reform programme be hastily developed and poorly implemented, the energy sector could experience a profound crisis which might restrain the country's economic growth and development for a number of years.

Evaluation of China's Approach

This review of China's energy security policy has shown that the government has placed great emphasis on maximising domestic production of oil and gas, on investing in overseas production, and on enhancing political links with exporting states supplemented by overseas aid and outward investment. These measures are characteristic of a 'strategic' rather than a 'market' approach to energy security.

China has been rather slow on a number of other fronts. The liberalisation of the internal energy markets has barely commenced, demand-side measures in the transport sector are largely absent, and emergency response systems are only now being put in place. Indeed, the government has yet to set up a specific agency responsible for security of oil supply, nor is there even a Ministry of Energy or equivalent. The current policy for enhancing the country's security of energy supply may be reasonably characterised as *ad hoc* and incomplete.[62]

China's current approach resembles aspects of Japan's strategy developed in the 1970s, except that it lacks the coherent measures to constrain oil demand and to develop emergency response capacity at an appropriate rate. It contrasts greatly with the current proposals of the EC and the US government, which emphasise a range of demand-side measures and of market mechanisms on the supply side, as well as a number of non-market actions such as improving emergency response systems and building political relations with exporters.

The willingness of China's government to put greater emphasis on market measures is constrained by a number of factors: the lack of understanding within China of how energy markets function; real technical and institutional obstacles to undertaking a rapid liberalisation of the energy sector; and, most importantly, a selection of parties such as the state petroleum companies whose interests are served by maintaining the status quo and taking a strategic approach to energy security.

For these reasons, China's current approach to energy security may seem rather old fashioned and better suited to the 1970s than to the first decade of the twenty-first century. It certainly involves the government, through the state banks, in considerable direct expenditure. Membership of the WTO should reinforce the growing liberalisation of China's economy, but liberalisation of the energy sector is likely to lag significantly.

As in most countries, energy policy in China is inseparable

from domestic and foreign politics.[63] Understanding this interaction requires us to examine the players in Chinese politics, how policy decisions are made, and how these decisions have been implemented in the context of China's international energy policy, especially for oil and gas. This is the subject of the next chapter.

Chapter 2

China's Energy Security Policymaking and Implementation

The previous chapter highlighted the ad hoc and incomplete character of China's energy policy and the tendency of the Chinese government to promote a strategic rather than market-oriented approach to ensuring security of energy supply. This approach, it was argued, is more characteristic of the statist and interventionist energy policies of the 1970s than the current more liberal and market-oriented orthodoxy. The principal objective of this chapter is to uncover why this strategic approach towards energy security policy is so prevalent in China. This involves an examination of the key actors in Chinese energy security policy, their preferences and interests, and how they interact in the process of policy formation and in making and implementing decisions. The first section identifies the most important actors in this area and their converging and diverging interests. This is followed by four case-studies which provide empirical evidence of policies which have been defined, promoted and then either implemented or shelved in the international quest for ensuring China's energy security. These case studies provide a means for opening up, even if partially, the complex and opaque nature of the 'black box' of Chinese decision making.

These four case studies focus on continental Asia and how China has approached the problem of development of the energy resources which are located in a broad east–west arc from the Russian Far East, to north-west China, Central Asia and the Middle East. There are two reasons for this focus. First, there is evidence that Chinese decision makers look at this broader region as a unity when considering energy security. This broader region represents, in one Chinese analyst's analogy, an 'energy belt' where most of China's future imports of oil and gas will come from and where most of the world's remaining supplies of oil and gas are to be found.[1] In addition, it is from the contiguous countries to the north and west of China where direct pipeline connections are possible. The second reason is that the energy-related decisions towards this region include significant political and foreign policy concerns as well as more strictly economic and efficiency considerations. As a result, these case-studies provide insights into how domestic politics and foreign policy influence decision making and the extent to which they promote a more strategic than market-oriented approach to energy security.

The Actors and Their Priorities

China's policy making has developed considerably from the Mao period when a rigidly centralised and hierarchic decision-making structure ensured that policies were imposed from above with almost no input from below. Since the opening up, initiated by Deng Xiaoping in 1978, a more liberalised policy-making environment has emerged which has provided more extensive consultation, a bargaining process between differing interest groups, and more careful monitoring of policy implementation.[2] Despite these advances, the absence of a clear process of political democratisation has meant that the policy-making process remains opaque and that key decisions still require the imprimatur of the top leadership of the Chinese Communist Party (CCP). The result is a complex and factionalised political system which Lieberthal and Oksenberg describe as involving a 'fragmented structure of authority'.[3] Seeking to uncover how policies are formed and decisions are made within this structure is inherently difficult.

When analysing China's energy security policy, the key actors which can be identified include:

- The top leadership of the party and government
- The military
- The relevant government departments

- The state petroleum companies.

Other more subsidiary actors might include:

- Provincial governments
- Think-tanks.

The top leadership of the party and government is formally repre-sented by the Politburo and by the State Council respectively. However, the key decision-making bodies where real power is concentrated are the smaller sub-groupings of the Standing Com-mittee of the Politburo (normally between five to seven members) and the inner cabinet of premier and vice premiers of the State Council (involving between five to ten members).[4] These bodies play a critical role in Chinese decision making since they ultimately approve all major decisions. Individuals within these bodies also play a crucial role since it is recognised that large projects will only get the necessary attention and approval at the highest levels if they gain the enthusiastic patronage of at least one of this small élite of top leaders.[5] Such personal intervention is often required to break through and transcend the otherwise fragmented and com-peting bureaucratic structures which can paralyse decision making.

The top leadership also naturally takes a leading role in defining the broad framework of China's policy objectives and the country's leading priorities in terms of domestic and foreign policy interests. As China enters the twenty-first century, three recent high-level policy decisions, all of which were taken in 2000, illustrate the current preoccupations of the Chinese leadership.[6] The first such policy decision was triggered by the shift of power in Taiwan from the long-time ruling party of the Kuomintang to the pro-independence Democratic Progressive Party in 2000. Tai-wan's internal development provoked a strategic reassessment in China of its Taiwan policy. In February 2000, the government issued a White Paper on Taiwan which indicated a hardening of China's posture and a greater willingness to use military force to ensure national reunification.[7] This shriller rhetoric was followed by a growing level of military preparedness, significant increases in military expenditure, and a clear shift towards a more official anti-American orientation which was clearly set out in a White Paper on Defence, also issued in 2000. Although in practice the

Chinese leadership recognises that reunification is a long-term ambition, the issue of Taiwan remains a central and obsessive preoccupation where the use of force cannot be ruled out.

The second major strategic decision in 2000 was the proclamation of the 'Develop the West' policy which sought to reorient China's regional economic development by allocating more resources to the poorer inland region.[8] This reflected the Chinese leadership's growing concern over the disparities in wealth between the dynamic coastal region and the stagnant and economically depressed regions in the northern and western interior. The third major decision was Jiang Zemin's articulation of the concept of the 'three representations' which argued that the future survival of the CCP required it to 'represent' the advanced forces of production, culture, and the interests of the people.[9] In layman's terms, this was directed towards the modernisation of the CCP through extending party membership beyond the traditional urban and rural proletariat to include members from business and the intelligentsia.[10] The sense among the Chinese leadership of the need to increase the legitimacy of the CCP, and to root out the endemic corruption within its ranks, has become particularly urgent given the generational shift of power in the top Chinese leadership which is widely predicted to take place during 2002 and 2003. [11]

These three strategic decisions highlight perhaps the most pressing current preoccupations of the Chinese leadership. They also provide insights into the main priorities and hierarchy of interests of the top leadership. At risk of considerable simplification, these can be identified as:

- Survival and regeneration of the CCP
- Social and political stability
- Economic development
- Integrity and unity of country, most notably the reunification of Taiwan
- Regional influence
- International status.

When examining Chinese energy security policy, the Chinese

leadership's interest is primarily engaged when such policy contributes to, or potentially conflicts with, these core priorities. Certainly, given the fact that sufficient supplies of energy are essential to economic development and thus to social and political stability, there is a generalised interest in energy security issues. However, as the case studies demonstrate, such interest is particularly evident when energy linkages potentially extend China's regional or international influence, such as in Russia, Central Asia and the Middle East. Similarly, the ways in which energy can help to undermine threats to national unity and to contribute to promoting social and political stability excite similar top-level engagement. The case study on Xinjiang and the decision to develop the West-to-East gas pipeline demonstrates this well.

For the military, the People's Liberation Army (PLA), energy security issues can be considered to assume even less of a priority than for the top civilian leadership. The PLA's priorities are focused primarily on national security, such as the perceived threat posed by the US along with the defence and promotion of China's territorial claims, most notably as regards to Taiwan and the South China Sea.[12] Energy security policy *per se* might not be of direct interest but where such energy issues become embroiled with territorial issues involving foreign powers, the military does gain an influential voice. For example, it was reportedly at the PLA's insistence, and against the advice of the Foreign Ministry, that the Senkaku/Diaoyu islands were explicitly referred to as part of China's territory in the 1992 legislation which clarified the Chinese claims in the South and East China Seas.[13] The result was significantly to politicise and internationalise China's oil exploration and development in the region, accentuating Japanese fears and concerns for its own energy security. Likewise, a number of the leaders of the PLA have reportedly also expressed reservations about the development of energy linkages with Russia which might lead to an over-dependence on Russian supplies.[14] The military is therefore a significant actor when energy issues impinge on national security concerns. However, the fact that there are, and will remain, sufficient indigenous supplies of oil to ensure China's war-fighting capability means that the military is not dependent on overseas supplies for its operational capability.

Among the multiplicity of government agencies which are involved in international policy making, the two most important in terms of energy supply are the departments of the State Development Planning Commission (SDPC) and the State Economic and Trade Commission (SETC). Between them, they formulate general economic policy and draw together the key components of energy policy. The competencies of these agencies were redefined in Spring 1998 in the context of a general reform of the operations of China's state-owned enterprises. The newly created Ministry of Land and Natural Resources (MLNR), which administers land use, also plays a significant if subordinate role.[15] In general terms, these reforms sought to consolidate the shift in the government's role from being a central planning agency, managing vertical, command and control relations, to a more modest regulatory and supervisory role which involves the management of horizontal, contractual relations.

In the energy sector, the most significant outcome of the 1998 reforms was to devolve the role of enterprise management from the government to the state petroleum companies. With the government ceasing to take day-to-day control of the running of these companies, its role was restructured to focus on policy formulation and regulation.[16] Policy formulation involves the setting of priorities and the development of a coherent framework for the operation of the energy market, such as a transparent system of pricing. The regulatory function involves the regulation of the market to ensure domestic competition and that there are not opportunities for collusion between the monopolistic state oil companies. In practice, these new responsibilities for government are demanding and require more complex and sophisticated systems and procedures than the earlier command-and-control functions.

Since 1998, this reformed governmental structure and regulatory framework has had some significant successes. Domestic oil prices have moved closer to international prices, though they continue to be fixed through a formula devised by SDPC. Greater competition in the domestic petroleum market has also been encouraged through redistributing the assets of the two major oil companies, China National Petroleum Company (CNPC) and the China National Petrochemical Corporation (Sinopec), and making them vertically integrated companies.[17] However, there remain a number of weaknesses in the current governmental regulatory structure. First, the respective functions and responsibilities of the SDPC, SETC and MNLR remain ill-defined and subject to much inter-departmental negotiation and politicking. Second, the fact that so many of the staff from these departments have been drawn from the state energy industries suggests that the separation of government from enterprise functions is far from complete. This potential source of collusion between government and companies is exacerbated by the understaffing of the government bodies which requires them to call on the state companies for additional help, thus giving the companies to unduly influence policy-making and regulation.[18] Finally, these problems are affected by a more general failure of the government to provide a broader and more comprehensive energy policy, which would promote the market-oriented aspects of an energy security policy, such as demand-side measures in the transport sector. It is the absence of a powerful actor within government promoting such 'market-driven' policies that significantly contributes to the success of the other actors identified in this section promoting more 'strategic' measures.

The state-owned petroleum companies remain the final major actors in energy security policy. In the 1980s, the government created three large oil companies: the CNPC, which was responsible for exploration and production; Sinopec, responsible for refining and marketing; and China National Offshore Oil Corporation (CNOOC), which controlled most of the off-shore oil business. In the 1998 reforms, the government reorganised CNPC and Sinopec to create two vertically integrated oil companies. In addition, all three companies have set up subsidiaries in the period 1999–2001 which were floated on the international stock markets and whose shares have been bought by foreign investors.[19] For the purposes of this study, the main actor among these companies is CNPC, and its partly floated subsidiary, PetroChina. Despite the 1998 reforms, CNPC continues to have a near-monopoly status as the national upstream oil and gas company, has an uncontested regional dominance in the North and West of the country, and has been given the principal mandate for exploration, investment and development overseas.

Though the state petroleum companies are nominally subordinate and separate from the government, they have considerable power and influence based on their importance to the national economy, their near-monopoly status despite the 1998 reforms, and their previous status as government departments or ministries.[20] Their new-found commercial opportunities and relative independence also creates tensions with their formal subordination to the government as state-owned enterprises. While both CNPC and PetroChina are under pressure to maximise profits, this is likely to be more seriously enforced at the partially privatised PetroChina. Conversely, CNPC is more susceptible than PetroChina to government pressure to address issues concerning energy security.

CNPC has been given the major role in fulfilling the government's target of raising the level of oil imports from overseas production to 50 million tonnes by 2010.[21] These objectives have, it should be added, been welcomed by CNPC executives since it contributes to their ambition to become international players, to strengthen their international presence in global markets and to consolidate their financial position. This internationalisation of CNPC, and the other oil companies, is also supported by the Chinese government as indirectly strengthening energy security through ensuring that China is not dependent on the large Western petroleum multinationals for all its energy imports.

However, the interests of the companies are not entirely coincident with those of the government. The companies themselves can use their monopoly of expertise and their political influence to justify their commercial interests in overseas investments through arguing that they serve the government's energy security objectives.[22] Conversely, the government's understanding of energy security, which appears to include the expectation that the oil companies will forego windfall profits when there are price-hikes on the international market, would clearly conflict with these companies' commercial interests.[23] In general, the domestic political and foreign policy interests of the government, which are critical variables in the conceptualisation of energy security, are not part of the same calculus of interests of the oil companies. Another complicating factor is the inherited social obligations of the state-owned oil companies which include a bloated work-force of 1.54

million, which has now been reduced to 500,000, significant debts, and unfunded pension obligations.[24] This gives the companies a domestic social and political role, which complicates their ambition to become commercial international players and to encourage Western investment and capital.

The final set of actors, which can only be considered to play a subordinate role in energy security policy, include the provincial governments and the specialist think-tanks. Although decisions regarding energy security are taken at the centre, regional governments constantly demand and seek to obtain greater autonomy, particularly in relation to their region's national resources, to trading with overseas parties and to determine tax policies.[25] These demands are likely to become more insistent with entry into the WTO, which is likely to increase rural development and accentuate the divide between the prosperous coastal regions and the poorer inland. The central government is also particularly sensitive to the security concerns of provinces bordering foreign countries, such as Xinjiang, Inner Mongolia and Heilongjiang, and will be influenced by the arguments of regional elites that energy linkages would ameliorate such security concerns.

Finally, the proliferation of think-tanks in China have increasingly focused on energy security issues. This illustrates the growing complexity and sophistication of the policy-making process in China. While these think-tanks are not truly independent from their respective sponsoring bodies, whether from government or industry, they do provide professional and expert advice and enable a more rational process of decision making. It is clear that the Chinese leadership increasingly uses the services of these think-tanks, which are mostly located in Beijing, to provide information and differing perspectives on key problems under consideration.[26] The fact that it was only in the early 1990s that think-tanks associated with foreign policy and strategic studies began to be interested in energy security illustrates how political and strategic factors have increasingly interacted with more strictly economic and energy considerations.

Xinjiang: The West-to-East Gas Pipeline
The first case-study which gives more concrete empirical ex-

pression of the interaction of the various actors identified above is the development of the oil and gas resources of the western Chinese province of Xinjiang Uighur Autonomous region (XUAR). CNPC, and latterly PetroChina, have been engaged in Xinjiang for the last 20 years and have made a series of oil and gas discoveries in the Tarim basin. During the 1980s, the government and CNPC held great expectations that these resources would preserve China's energy self-sufficiency through supplementing the depleting oil reserves in the ageing oil fields of northern China. However, subsequent exploration proved to be disappointing and resulted in a substantial reduction in the estimates of the expected reserves.[27] In addition, the government was reluctant to support the major investment needed to develop these fields and transport the oil and gas to markets in the east of the country. The main reason was that the high costs of exploration, development and transportation made the reserves in Xinjiang relatively uncompetitive. As a consequence, in the mid-1990s the government encouraged CNPC to invest overseas and to secure cheaper supplies from foreign sources. In Spring 2000 this relative disinterest in Xinjiang was reversed by the decision to build a west-to-east gas pipeline from the Tarim basin to Shanghai as a flagship project within the 'Develop the West' programme.

The factors behind this sharp change in approach resulted from a significant convergence of economic, political, domestic and foreign policy interests which has forged a consensus among the various Chinese interest groups. Political pressures, which include domestic, foreign and strategic concerns, have been the most significant factors which have overridden the continuing questions of the economic viability and efficiency of the project. Independent analysts highlight the fact that, though this pipeline is as long as the Yamal pipeline from Siberia to Western Europe, there is an absence of substantial gas markets en route and the gas supplied will have to compete with potentially cheaper LNG supplies, possible supplies from eastern Siberia, and from China's abundant coal supplies.[28] However, these economic concerns have been clearly overridden by a high-level political decision, which has the personal imprimatur of the Chinese leadership, including the support of Jiang Zemin and Zhu Rongji.[29] The decision does, therefore, express the full weight and prestige of the highest levels of the Chinese political establishment.

A number of political factors have contributed to this shift in priorities towards the energy resources of Xinjiang. First, there is the increasing geopolitical importance that Xinjiang has gained since the end of the Cold War. This vast and thinly populated province, which is about half the size of India, has always had military and geopolitical significance.[30] It has traditionally acted as a strategic buffer against attack from potential external aggressors coming from the mountains and steppes north-west of China and has been the site for nuclear tests and large-scale military exercises. During the Sino-Soviet Cold War, when the Soviet Union was the main external threat, Xinjiang remained hermetically sealed from its immediate neighbours and was left relatively under-developed. With the disintegration of the Soviet Union, the Chinese government opened up the borders of Xinjiang for trade with the newly independent states of Central Asia. While such linkages were viewed as essential for promoting the development of the region, they also left Xinjiang more vulnerable to external forces and dynamics which, it was believed in Beijing, could threaten China's territorial integrity. A particular concern, in this regard, has been the growing influence and penetration of the US in Central Asia. The process of NATO enlargement, which has brought the Central Asian states in the Partnership for Peace programme, and NATO's intervention in Kosovo intensified fears that US military and political power was encroaching on China's immediate borders. The large-scale American intervention into Afghanistan in response to the terrorist attack of 11 September has only increased Chinese nervousness of the US presence in Central Asia.[31]

These geopolitical concerns have been exacerbated by the rising strength of secessionist sentiment and ethnic minority discontent in the region. Of the 17.4 million population in Xinjiang, the Turkic Central Asian ethnic groups represent a clear majority, with approximately 8 million Uighurs, 1.5 million Kazakhs, 200,000 Kyrgyz and 60,000 Tajiks. These minorities feel clearly differentiated from, and often resentful towards, the predominantly migrant ethnic Han Chinese population, who represent roughly 37% of the population. Throughout the 1990s, there have serious incidents of ethnic unrest. In 1990, there were riots in the town of Baren and, in 1997, these were followed by similar unrest in Yining.[32] In 1998, Chinese officials recognised that there were 70 serious incidents causing more than 380 fatalities. In September 2001, an explosion in Urumqi caused 67 deaths which many suspected, though officially denied by the Chinese authorities, was instigated by separatist forces.

The Chinese authorities have also been greatly concerned by the linkages between these ethnically based movements, the other Central Asian states and the broader Middle Eastern and Muslim world. Uighur organisations have proliferated throughout Central Asia, the Middle East and in the West. The predilection for some of these groups to engage in terrorist activity has been confirmed by the presence of Uighur fighters who were trained in al-Qaeda camps in Afghanistan.[33] Although the Uighur-based movements do not have the same international profile as the Tibetan organisations, it can be argued that the Chinese government perceives this threat to be of equal if not greater significance. There is considerable fear that continued Uighur unrest could lead to a Kurdish-style law enforcement problem which could undermine investor confidence in the region and weaken the government's claims to legitimacy and respectability.[34] In a worst case scenario, there are even fears of a Kosovo-style external intervention into the region.[35]

These political and strategic concerns have been some of the factors which have contributed to the commitment to the 'Develop the West' programme of which the west-to-east pipeline represents one of a number of large-scale infrastructure projects. This programme is not, though, primarily focused on external threats to China's national integrity. Its principal purpose is to consolidate domestic social and political stability, and the legitimacy of the government, through reversing the widening economic divide between the coastal provinces and the stagnating central and western regions.[36] In addition, development of these relatively backward regions is vital for giving momentum to sluggish domestic demand and the further success of economic reforms. The demands of WTO membership have only added to the sense of urgency in the shift of developmental priorities to the West.[37]

Economic development, therefore, has been the key long-term vehicle through which the Chinese government believes it can strengthen its control of Xinjiang, suppress secessionist tensions and discourage external intervention. These political concerns have undoubtedly contributed to the decision to go ahead with the west-to-east gas pipeline. But, a number of energy-related factors also probably helped to seal the decision. First, there was the pressing need to bring onstream substantial supplies of natural gas to support the government's policy of promoting gas use in China. The first wave of supply could be sourced from the Ordos basin in northern China. The choice that the government faced was whether the next wave would come from east Siberia (the Kovykta field near Irkutsk) which is widely accepted to be potentially profitable, or from the less commercially viable Tarim basin. The fact that the gas from Xinjiang offered greater security of supply, and the political and contractual problems which threatened to delay the Irkutsk development, swung decision makers in favour of the Tarim basin. Secondly, CNPC and PetroChina would have strongly lobbied the government in favour of the pipeline so that they could recoup some of their 20 years of exploration investment in the Tarim basin. Finally, by taking the west-to-east pipeline all the way to the coast, the Chinese government could fairly claim that the 'Develop the West' programme was providing a direct benefit to the coastal provinces through the provision of clean energy.

The conclusion to be drawn from this case-study is that the decision to construct the west-to-east gas pipeline was not based purely on energy or economic concerns. Energy security, and the interests of CNPC/PetroChina, were not sufficient justification for going ahead with this project, whose economic rationality remains controversial. It was only when political concerns, engaging the interest and commitment of the top leadership, were added to the equation that a consensus could be reached among all the major actors. The decision of the west-to-east pipeline has to be set, therefore, in this wider context of domestic, security and foreign policy making among China's domestic actors.

Central Asia: Gas from Turkmenistan and Oil from Kazakhstan

As the previous section has already argued, the disintegration of the Soviet Union transformed the geopolitical situation in Central Asia and posed new political and security challenges for the Chinese government. Initially, Chinese engagement was limited to establishing diplomatic relations with the newly independent countries and to promoting bilateral economic ties. It was only with the visit by Premier Li Peng in April 1994 to the Central Asian states that a higher-level political dynamic was initiated. One of the most significant commitments that Li Peng made during his visit was for the construction of a gas pipeline to connect the gas fields of Turkmenistan with China.[38] This proposal had been energetically promoted by Turkmen President Saparmurat Niyazov in two earlier visits to Beijing where he had apparently gained the support of Jiang Zemin. In 1996, CNPC, Exxon and Mitsubishi completed a feasibility study which projected that the overall cost of the pipeline would be about $12bn.[39] The enormous projected cost of the pipeline, the problem of raising the capital and the inherent political risk of a pipeline, which would traverse both Uzbekistan and Kazakhstan, has meant that little progress has been made, and is likely to be made in the near future.

The reasons why the Chinese government was emboldened to make this commitment reflected the primacy given to political and strategic concerns over economic considerations. In the internal policymaking process, it was reportedly foreign policy and strategic studies interest groups, newly aware of the need for China's energy import needs, who convinced the Chinese leadership to ignore the more cautious and sceptical views of the energy and economic analysts.[40] The commitment was also made at the same time as a growing Western interest in exploring and developing the energy resources of the Caspian region. The Chinese leadership was concerned that it might lose out in this new 'Great Game', which sought to fill the strategic vacuum caused by Russia's withdrawal from the region. The way in which the pipeline could consolidate Chinese influence in Central Asia more generally, while also providing for China's energy security interests by diversifying supplies from the Gulf region, added to the attractiveness of a bold Chinese intervention. CNPC undoubtedly supported this geopolitical and strategic approach adopted by the government, though its interests were more narrowly defined by the prospect of the Turkmen pipeline adding to the justification of a west–east gas pipeline from Xinjiang to the coastal regions.[41] In the end, though, the policy implementation phase highlighted the economic irrationality and high political risk of the pipeline and essentially killed off the prospects for its construction.

This early foray did not, though, discourage further Chinese involvement in the Central Asian energy sector. In 1997, a far more serious and substantive commitment was made by CNPC in Kazakhstan when it won the right to develop two oil fields in Akhtubinsk and an oilfield in Uzen. In its successful bid for the Akhtubinsk oilfields, CNPC beat off competition from Texaco, Amoco and Russia's Yuzhnimost through pledging to invest $4.3bn over 20 years. In addition, the Chinese promised to build a 6,000 km oil pipeline from Akhtubinsk to China with an estimated cost of $3.5bn.[42] Six years later, though, in a rather similar process to that involving the Turkmen pipeline, little progress has been made on any of these projects. Again, the move by China into Kazakhstan appears to have been driven as much or more by political and strategic considerations than by energy concerns. In economic terms, the construction of a 6,000 km oil pipeline makes little commercial sense when the alternative is to buy from international markets and have the oil delivered by ship to the coast.

The political concerns included fears of ethnic and religious linkages between Kazakhs and Uighurs on both sides of the border fomenting unrest in Xinjiang. The Chinese energy linkage with Kazakhstan was perceived as a useful instrument to encourage the Kazakh government to crack down on such groups. The apparent weakening of Russian control in the region, and the economic, political and military penetration of the West and the US, strengthened the arguments for building close economic and political links with Kazakhstan. In addition, the fact that Kazakhstan was an immediate neighbour with substantial petroleum resources provided China with one of the best prospects of having an overseas oil supply which could be secured under Chinese ownership and control. This was perceived to conform with China's energy security strategy. CNPC was also in favour of the project as it would have expected to see substantial benefit flowing from the development of the overseas production as well as the construction of the pipeline which, among other things, would have allowed them to develop more of their marginally commercial oil fields in the Tarim basin.

As with the Turkmen project, economic considerations have been the most significant reasons for China's failure to develop its energy investments in Kazakhstan. First was the sudden fall of international oil prices in 1997 which made all petroleum investments in Central Asia look unattractive. Then came the reorganisation of China's petroleum industry in 1998 which gave CNPC the opportunity to invest in a range of more attractive activities within China which had previously been off-limits, such as oil refining and marketing and gas distribution. An increasing emphasis on the need to make profits further reduced CNPC's enthusiasm for its Kazakh projects. Finally, CNPC became increasingly frustrated at the administrative and fiscal obstacles it was encountering doing business in Kazakhstan, which was mirrored by Kazakh disenchantment at CNPC's perceived failure to honour its contractual obligations.[43]

Political developments also contributed to China's disinclination to engage more fully with Kazakhstan's energy sector. In the late 1990s, the reassertion of a more sustained and energetic Russian engagement in Central Asia changed the strategic calculus. This revival of Russian influence was due to the more effective and dynamic policies of President Vladimir Putin and the recognition among the Central Asian states of their security dependence on Russia for dealing with the growing Islamist and terrorist threats emerging from Afghanistan. With this shift in Russia's geopolitical favour in Central Asia, the Chinese government was more cautious in promoting policies, such as those in the energy field, which might be considered unfavourably in Moscow. The increasing convergence in strategic outlook between China and Russia, which included common views on the need to quell Islamist and ethnic unrest and to limit Western penetration, also fostered a greater Chinese confidence in supporting Russia as the principal security guarantor in the region. China's success in forming a regional organisation, which was initially called the 'Shanghai 5' but was redesignated in 2001 as the Shanghai Cooperation Organisation (SCO), contributed to alleviating Beijing's security concerns.[44] The SCO, whose members include Russia, China and all the Central Asian states except Turkmenistan, initially focused on border issues and confidence-building measures but subsequently developed into a body with a clear security remit, issuing in 2000 the 'Shanghai Convention on Fighting Terrorism, Separatism and Extremism'. The Chinese authorities also found the Central Asian states receptive to their demands for a clamp-down on Uighur and other groups seeking to destabilise Xinjiang.[45] Indeed, the Kazakh government was just as keen to repress Uighur secessionist groups since they potentially represent as much a threat to their own territorial integrity, given that an independent Uighurstan would also make claims on Kazakh territory.

The conclusion that can be drawn is that by the middle of 2001 economic reality, combined with the emergence of other instruments for dealing with China's security concerns in Central Asia, had undermined the earlier politically-driven enthusiasm for developing the energy resources of Kazakhstan. As a consequence, the CNPC's investment plans in Kazakhstan, though not dead, were nearly dormant. However, it should not be excluded that political and strategic developments might evolve to revive Chinese interest. The events of 11 September have triggered a re-evaluation by the Chinese government with energy security assuming an increasingly important prominence for the top leadership. They might yet decide that the current dependence on the Gulf for oil supplies is excessive, that a stronger Chinese presence in Central Asia is required to counter-balance the growing US influence, and that the Kazakhstan oil pipeline should be constructed, regardless of cost.

Russia: A Source of Oil and Gas

The relatively untapped energy resources of eastern Siberia and the Russian Far East are the main alternatives, in territory contiguous to China, to the supplies from Central Asia. Whenever the Chinese leadership promoted their ambition of developing energy linkages with Central Asia, they were also careful to counter-balance this with assurances of their interest in developing supplies from Russia. Thus, when Li Peng made his commitment in 1994 for a gas pipeline from Turkmenistan, he added that China was similarly committed to developing a pipeline from the Kovykta gas fields near to Irkutsk.[46] The salience of Sino-Russian energy connections has only increased as the political relationship has assumed greater significance and substantive content. Viewed in the perspective of the last two decades, there has been a remarkable transformation in these relations, from a highly militarised and antagonistic relationship in the mid-1980s to an initial thawing in the late 1980s and to the establishment of a 'constructive partnership' in 1994 which was upgraded to a 'strategic partnership' two years later. This culminated in July 2001 with the signing of a treaty of friendship and cooperation.[47]

The principal impetus behind this dramatic *rapprochement*, beside the common resolve to avoid the damaging costs of the earlier militarised conflict, has been a geopolitical strategic convergence between the two countries in opposition to the global dominance and influence of the US. Both countries have felt marginalised in the post-Cold War world and have increasingly perceived the US to be pursuing policies antithetical to their national security interests, whether this be through NATO enlargement, National Missile Defence, penetration into Central Asia, or support for secessionist forces such as in Taiwan or Chechnya. In such a strategic environment, Chinese and Russian leaders have made great efforts to resolve their mutual differences so as to offer a common front against the perceived threat of US hegemony. There is recognition, though, that the relationship will lack enduring and strong foundations unless it is underpinned by a vibrant and dynamic economic dimension. This also has a specific regional urgency since the Russian Far East has been in terminal economic decline during the post-Soviet period and its economic and social regeneration is critically dependent on the region's integration into the dynamic East Asian markets.

The trade and investment component of the relationship has, though, been slow to develop. During the 1990s, bilateral trade has grown to reach $8bn in 2000 but this contrasts with the $115bn of trade between China and the US.[48] Arms sales from Russia to

China have been the most significant aspect of this trade with China's ambitions of military modernisation highly dependent on the sale of arms, the licensing of production facilities and military technology transfer from Russian suppliers. In August 1999, Russia and China reportedly signed arms agreements of more than $15bn for the following five years, representing about $2.5bn per annum.[49] Beyond arms, energy remains potentially the most significant sector to expand the levels of trade. Eastern Siberia and the Russian Far East possess vast untapped accumulations of oil and gas which are far larger than can be consumed by the declining local population.[50] The nearest market for these fields is Northeast Asia, including Korea, Japan and China. But only China has the potential to provide a large market in the relatively near future. For Russia, oil and gas exports promise to address the desperate need to raise its GDP and exports and to develop its impoverished eastern provinces. For China, such imports promise to provide relatively cheap and reliable supplies, strengthening energy security through diversification away from the Gulf, and underpinning the strategic relationship with Russia.

In the long term, gas is the most significant resource in eastern Siberia and the Russian Far East and should be the principal fuel to flow to China.[51] The Kovykta fields near Irkutsk have been under evaluation by BP and CNPC since the mid-1990s, with the idea of transporting the gas by pipeline to north-east China. It is widely recognised that economically this is the most viable of all the large-scale overseas gas projects that have been considered by the Chinese government. To the north-east of Irkutsk lie the potentially vast, but not fully proven, reserves of the Sakha Republic, which could potentially be connected to any gas pipeline from Kovytka. Additional sources of gas exist in the Sakhalin region, though these are not currently destined for China, and in western Siberia, from where a pipeline has been proposed which would run south-eastwards into northern Xinjiang. Despite the political desire for these gas projects to go ahead, little has happened. The decision to build the domestic west-to-east gas pipeline, and the factors behind this decision described earlier, have overtaken the plans for a gas connection with Russia. Energy security concerns, which appear to have included the disquiet of the PLA to over-dependence on Russia, might also have contributed to this decision.[52]

The Chinese government was keen, though, not to leave their Russian partners empty-handed. At a relatively late stage, the Russian gas monopoly, Gazprom, was invited to join the consortium, including Shell, PetroChina and the Hong Kong and China Gas Company, which in early 2002 appears to be the strongest candidate to construct the west-to-east pipeline, though still to be finalised.[53] In July 2001, hot on the heels of the treaty of friendship and cooperation, an agreement was signed between Chinese and Russian parties to construct an oil pipeline.[54] This would run from the oil fields of Angarsk, by chance also near Irkutsk in east Siberia, eastwards to the Daqing oil field in Heilongjiang Province in the far north-east of China. Until late 2000, little attention had been given to the prospect of constructing oil pipelines from Russia to China. The attraction of this option for China reflects a number of factors beyond the political benefits of consolidating the strategic partnership with Russia. The route chosen avoids Mongolia and the risks associated with any pipeline running across third countries and the oil pipeline could potentially be supplemented by a gas pipeline from the Kovytka fields, if a decision was finally made in its favour. The pipeline will also be connected directly into existing infrastructure at the Daqing field, which traditionally has underpinned the country's oil industry, but where production is now set to decline. The oil imported from Russia will progressively displace Daqing oil and feed into the pipelines and refineries in north-east China. Such an arrangement will prevent a rapid closure of these facilities, with consequent economic losses for CNPC and PetroChina and an incremental unemployment burden for local and central governments. In addition, the use of existing infrastructure will reduce the lead time and the capital investment needed for the project.

This first major cooperative energy project between Russia and China demonstrates the resolve of both countries to consolidate an energy component to their strategic partnership. It also indicates a Chinese concern to maintain the confidence of their Russian partners which might have been undermined by the decision to prioritise the gas pipeline from Xinjiang rather than from eastern Siberia. Furthermore, the Angarsk-Daqing oil pipeline demonstrates the Chinese concern with economic considerations and ensuring that the interests of the key actors are engaged, most notably in this case CNPC, PetroChina and local and central government.

The Middle East: A Crucial Source of Oil

The final case study, China's growing interest in the oil supplies from the Middle East and the Gulf region, differs from the previous cases in three critical aspects. First, these supplies are located in regions which are not territorially contiguous with the Chinese mainland and thus need to be transported on tankers through sea-lines of communication which are policed by external forces, most notably the US navy. The security implications of this are foremost in Chinese strategic considerations with the realisation that there is no prospect of changing this security vulnerability in any radical way in the short-to-medium-term. Second, there is the economic and geological reality that, given China's rising domestic demand for oil and the location of most of the world's proven reserves in the Gulf region, the Chinese will inevitably become more dependent on oil supplies from this region, however many financial resources are devoted to diversifying supplies. Third, the Middle East is a region where China's geopolitical and political presence has traditionally been marginal and where again there is little prospect of reversing this situation and genuinely challenging other external powers, most critically the US but also the major West European powers and even Russia.

In the Middle East, therefore, it is economic and energy-related interests which are the principal drivers of China's foreign policy and diplomatic initiatives and not, as is predominantly the case in the previous case studies, the other way around. Although there do exist significant political and strategic interests, such as the perceived need to inhibit the flow of political extremism from the Middle East to Central Asia and Xinjiang, these are subordinate to the more urgent requirement to assure access to oil supplies and to promoting the prospects for Chinese companies to explore and invest in the region.[55]

On a general diplomatic level, these energy-related objectives have led to the Chinese leadership making a concerted effort to strengthen China's political and strategic presence in the region. This has involved reversing the legacy of China's revolutionary past when the main objective was to support radical extremist movements in an attempt to out-bid the Soviet Union.[56] The consequence of these earlier policies had meant China lacked diplomatic relations with many of the moderate regimes in the region, including Israel, Saudi Arabia and the other Gulf states. The re-establishment of diplomatic relations with Saudi Arabia in 1990 represented the culmination of the efforts to secure China's diplomatic presence with all the states in the region. In the aftermath of the Gulf War of 1990–1991, during which China adopted a notably passive stance, Beijing sought to establish its credentials as a responsible international citizen, supportive of regional peace and stability.[57] It became a party to the peace process which had been established at the Madrid Conference of 1991 and participated in five multilateral working groups, chairing the water committee which sought to reduce the tensions relating to water supplies in the Middle East region.[58]

To pursue its more specific energy-related interests, the Chinese government has promoted a three-pronged approach. First, it has engaged in a diplomatic offensive to secure long-term supply arrangement with key oil-exporting Gulf states.[59] High-level visits by Chinese leaders to Saudi Arabia, which culminated in Jiang Zemin's 1999 state visit where he pronounced a 'strategic oil partnership' between the two countries, saw volumes of oil exports rising from 60,000 barrels per day (bpd) in 1996 to 350,000 bpd in 2000 on a 10-year contract.[60] Likewise, agreements were reached for Iran's exports to increase from 20,000 bpd in 1995 to 200,000 bpd in 2000. Similar arrangements have been made with Oman and Yemen as well as with other Gulf producers. The second prong has been the aggressive intervention of Chinese oil companies to gain rights to invest and develop oil fields in the region. In 1997, in the same period as the CNPC's entry into Kazakhstan, the company made substantial commitments to develop oil fields in Sudan and Iraq.[61] Both these projects were controversial given the Sudanese government's poor human rights record and the international sanctions regime on Iraq. The production-sharing contract with Iraq to develop the al-Ahdab field located in Central Iraq was also jointly signed by CNPC and Norinco, a partially independent Chinese arms company, raising concerns over whether an arms-for-oil agreement had been reached.[62] China has also clearly expressed its interest in field developments in Iran, though nothing has as yet been finalised.

The third part of China's strategy has been to encourage counter-investments by Gulf petroleum countries in the Chinese refining and marketing sectors. The objectives of this are to consolidate Sino-Gulf relations by giving the Gulf states an opportunity to gain access to these markets and allowing China to overcome domestic capital bottlenecks.[63] Thus, the Chinese government agreed in principle to Saudi Aramco being involved in joint ventures and approved its construction of a refinery in Qingdao, despite resistance from Sinopec. However, five years later in 2002, little progress has been made on this project.

The overall consequence of all these energy-related agreements in the Middle East and the Gulf is that China has a much higher geo-economic profile in the region. Its political presence, and its strategic interest in the region, have also inevitably increased in significance. But, given its continued political weakness compared to the other major external actors in the region, Chinese decision makers continue to face a number of strategic dilemmas. There is the question of whether China should strengthen its ties to oil-producing states in the region which have antagonistic relations with the US, such as Iran and Iraq, and to continue its policy of promoting arms sales to such states. The more general dilemma is how China should respond to its inevitable dependence on the US for the security of the Persian Gulf and the sealines of communication and whether it should offer *de facto* support for US policies or seek to counter-balance US dominance through coalitions with countries such as Russia and Iran.[64] These dilemmas are assessed more fully in the next chapter on the strategic implications of China's energy diplomacy.

Conclusion

This chapter has sought to identify the key actors in China's energy security policy and to analyse a number of the most significant commitments that have been made towards major oil and gas projects. In the case studies examined, the Middle East was distinctive as being the region which poses both great opportunities and great vulnerabilities. On the one hand, it is potentially the solution to China's energy needs since it is the region with the most abundant and cheapest sources of supply but, on the other, it poses the greatest energy security problems since the threats to these supplies are perceived among Chinese decision makers to be greatest. In the Middle East, economic logic and necessity drives political decision making. The economic and political factors are more finely balanced as regards the oil and gas resources in Xinjiang, Central Asia and Russia since the economic costs are higher and the political risk factors are perceived to be less, if still significant.

The two major commitments made so far – the west-to-east gas pipeline and the Angarsk-Daqing oil pipeline – are the outcomes of many years of complex negotiations both between the key domestic interest groups and with the relevant foreign countries. The degree of caution manifest in the lengthy policymaking process reflected the need to gain a consensus among the key domestic actors. It also illustrates the willingness of the Chinese government, in the policy implementation stage, critically to assess policy commitments which were originally driven by political and strategic considerations so as to ensure that they conform to basic conditions of economic viability and are responsive to shifts in China's strategic and foreign policy objectives. Thus, the decision to forge ahead with the west-to-east pipeline was driven by the determination of the top leadership, supported by the military, provincial governments and other governmental agencies, to promote economic development and to ensure social and political stability in the region, and by the state oil companies' commercial interests. The decision to prioritise a Russian project over one from Central Asia, despite the strong commitments made in particular to Kazakhstan, illustrates the shift in Chinese foreign policy towards the need to cement relations with Russia along with a reassessment of the economic and political risks of energy linkages with Central Asia.

In general, Chinese policy making, particularly in the policy implementation stage, is characterised by caution and careful assessments of the relative costs and benefits, particularly where third countries are concerned. Nevertheless, the decisions taken conform to an energy security policy which is dominated by strategic measures and where the government is willing to assume considerable potential costs to achieve its energy security objectives. The key actors in the policy-making process have a predominantly 'strategic' orientation and there is a notable absence of a significant input from interest groups who might promote supply-side and more market-driven solutions to ensuring energy security. As is argued throughout this Paper, this absence might be considered to be the greatest potential threat to China's energy security. Moreover, the fact that this predominantly strategic approach is likely to remain a feature, even if potentially a declining feature, of China's approach to its growing energy needs, raises a number of important challenges for the global energy markets and the interests of Western and other external actors. It is to these broader geopolitical and strategic concerns that the next chapter addresses itself.

Chapter 3

The Strategic Implications of China's Energy Needs

The first chapter provided an account of China's energy needs and the policies promoted to ensure security of supply. The second chapter sought to explain the policy-making process, identifying the main actors involved in decision making for energy security policy, and describing the process through which certain key decisions were made, such as the west-to-east gas pipeline, the energy investments in Central Asia and Russia, and the energy-driven relationship with key Middle Eastern oil-exporting countries. The main conclusion is that Chinese policy is driven by a clear concern about increasing energy vulnerability which has led to decisions which at times prioritise geopolitical and strategic considerations over economic and efficiency concerns. This chapter assesses the implications of China's evolving energy security policy for Western strategy towards China and the wider Asia-Pacific region.

There is nothing unusual or necessarily anti-Western about China adopting an energy security policy which is driven by geopolitical and strategic concerns. Ever since the oil price shocks of the 1970s, all modern industrialised states, irrespective of their ideological orientation, have been greatly exercised by their perceived vulnerability to energy supplies from the volatile and unstable Persian Gulf region. Such concerns have only intensified in the aftermath of the 11 September terrorist attacks in the US. Japan, for example, has been highly sensitive about its energy dependence and has consistently adopted a strategic-oriented energy security policy but has remained firmly wedded to its alliance with the US and the West.[1] China's case is clearly different not because of its energy security concerns but because it is emerging as a great power independent from, and broadly antagonistic towards, the Western-dominated international order and with a political elite whose geostrategic intentions are the subject of considerable debate among Western analysts.

The broad outline of this debate is well-known. There is, on the one hand, the classical realist view of China as an emerging hegemonic power with a value system inimical to Western norms and with policies, such as the modernisation of its military forces, which promote revisionist and anti-status quo ambitions. The alternative more benign liberal interdependence view sees China as a country which is inexorably being integrated into the global economy and into a gradual accommodation to the norms of international political behaviour.[2] Traditionally, the main focus of this debate has been on such issues as China's military build-up, its human rights record, and its expansive claims to Taiwan and the South China Seas. The energy dimension has only recently been added to the debate, quite naturally as China has only become dependent on imports since 1993.

Despite its recent inclusion, the energy question has not helped to resolve the debate. The 'China threat' school can point to how energy linkages are binding together the anti-Western Sino-Russian relationship; how it is preparing the groundwork for Chinese hegemony in Central Asia; and how it is promoting an obstructionist presence in the Middle East with Chinese arms and missiles being sold in exchange for oil and gas supplies. The Chinese naval build-up and belligerence in the South and East China Seas has also been linked to the potential energy resources located there. More broadly, the Asian competition for the supposedly scarce energy resources from the Persian Gulf, and along the critical sea-lines of communication, is seen as a potential catalyst for wider regional confrontations between the largest oil-importing countries in the region – India, China and Japan – and with the main external regional security guarantor, the US.[3]

The alternative liberal 'engagement' school provides a very different projection of how energy considerations might affect

broader geostrategic developments. Instead of conflict and confrontation, energy linkages are viewed as mechanisms which
potentially promote cooperation and integration. Thus, the anti-
Western orientation of the Sino-Russian *rapprochement* is over-
looked in favour of the security benefits of the overcoming of the
enmity between Russia and China and the ways in which energy
linkages can provide a material foundation for the continued
improvement of relations. Broader multilateral energy cooperation
can also be viewed as a natural and necessary response to the
common Asian concern about the threat of oil supplies from the
Middle East. A number of ambitious proposals have already been
made for developing a North-East Asian gas pipeline grid, which
would connect Russia, China, Japan and South Korea.[4] Much as the
European integration process was initiated through common policy towards coal and steel, so common East Asian policy over oil
and gas could conceivably provide the catalyst for overcoming
cultural, geographical and political divisions.

It is clearly difficult to predict how the energy variable in
China's foreign policy will influence China's geostrategic interaction with the international system and the implications for Western
policies. As with much in international relations, the intentions of
the actors, and most critically the mutual perceptions of these
intentions, will play a critical role in determining future outcomes.
China clearly feels highly vulnerable with its emerging energy
dependencies and its energy security policy will be influenced by
the degree to which it perceives more general Western policy as
seeking to engage, constrain or contain. Likewise, Western strategy
towards China will be influenced by the degree to which China's
quest for energy security appears to conflict with Western strategic
interests. China's energy security policy is therefore inevitably
affected by the broader strategic context and health of Sino-US and
Sino-Western relations.

While taking these qualifications into account, the argument
of this chapter supports the liberal interdependence view and
contends that the more alarming projections of how China's energy
security policy may influence China's behaviour are generally
exaggerated. Indeed, it is argued that the Chinese preference for
adopting a strategic rather than a market-driven approach to

energy security is more a threat to its own development than to the interests of the West.

This argument is pursued through a closer examination of some of the more alarmist and realist-inspired prognoses of China's energy policy. These prognoses are then critically assessed to determine whether they are valid and the extent to which they should be taken seriously by Western policy makers. In general, the assessments made qualify the more exaggerated fears and suggest a greater understanding of the strategic nuances and implications of Chinese energy security policy. The chapter examines the following five potentially alarming scenarios in China's energy policy:

- That it will lead to oil scarcity and competition between states over energy resources
- That it will lead to military competition and potential confrontation
- That it will have serious geopolitical implications in East Asia detrimental to Western interests
- That it will lead to more obstructionist Chinese behaviour in the Middle East.
- That it will contribute to China's domestic problems.

Implications for Global Oil Supplies

Asia is already playing a central role in global oil markets and will only become more dominant. This dynamic can be seen in the fact that, in 2000, 92% of global net growth in oil consumption came from Asia as against 68% in 1999.[5] China will be a critical element in this. As identified in Chapter 1, China's oil consumption will increase from 200 million tonnes to 300 million tonnes by 2010 and imports will constitute 50% of the supply in 2010 as against 30% currently. The broader picture is that Asia is projected to import 1,000 million tonnes per year by 2010, twice as much as the US now imports. This high level of imports is the outcome of Asia possessing only 4% of the world's proven reserves while constituting 50% of the world's population. The developing countries in Asia, most notably China and India, will be the driving forces leading to a projected 50% increase in energy demand by the year 2020. In addition, the majority of these energy supplies will come from the Gulf Middle East. Asia will be dependent for 80% of its oil supplies from the Gulf, as against about 35% for Europe and 20% for the US. Likewise, almost all of the gas exports from the Middle East will be directed towards Asia.[6]

From a classical realist perspective, it is not difficult for a geostrategist to depict some worrying and alarming scenarios from these figures and projections. Such scenarios can become even starker if an assumption is made that future oil supply will not meet demand and that there is likely to be an energy crisis in the reasonably near future. In this context, the rising oil prices and the struggle for preferential arrangements with petroleum-exporting states can be projected to have a particularly damaging impact on Asia. The negative geostrategic implications, leading to direct competition and conflict between the major Asian importing states, can be readily extrapolated.

Such conflict-ridden scenarios depend on the validity of the assumption of the future scarcity of oil supplies and the resultant inability of the energy markets to provide for the needs of China and other Asian states. There is, though, little evidence that such an assumption is valid. Certainly, as has been the case throughout the past century, there are prophets of doom who argue that oil is running out and that a major energy crisis is just around the corner.[7] However, such projections have been proven wrong in the past and are likely to be proven just as wrong in the future.[8] Despite the fears of an oil crunch during the past 30 years, there has actually been a secular decline in oil prices and, in the 1990s, annual oil demand increased globally by 400 million tonnes for which supplies were found without difficulty.[9] These achievements have been due to an increasingly globalised and efficient oil market, the creation of a well-established physical trading system and, perhaps most importantly, the continuous technological advances which have meant that substantial additional reserves have been recovered. Most recently, these discoveries have been made in the deep waters of the South Atlantic and the Gulf of Mexico. Some analysts, such as Michael Lynch, even argue that it is nonsensical to suggest that the 'world is running out of oil' since reserves are determined by the interaction of technological progress, government policies and the price people are willing to pay for oil products. Since future prices cannot be known so reserves cannot be quantified.[10]

The International Energy Agency is officially rather more cautious and argues that conventional oil resources are likely to become scarcer from 2010–2020. However, the increased scarcity of conventional oil resources will just mean that it will become commercially viable to develop alternative fuels and non-conventional oil resources – such as heavy oil, tar sands and oil shale – for which there are known to be massive reserves. Just as the stone age did not end because man ran out of stones, so the oil age will not end because man runs out of oil resources. As long as international markets are permitted to operate efficiently and the investments are made to bring new supplies to the market, China and other Asian countries can be reassured that that their energy needs will be met, so long as they have the capital to pay for them. OPEC and the oil-producing states have a similar interest in ensuring uninterrupted and adequate supplies to meet demand since they know from experience that any significant disruptions, or excessive price hikes, only accelerates the diversification of supplies and the development of alternative fuels.

This does not mean, though, that there are no reasons for China and other Asian states to be worried about their increasing dependence on Middle East supplies. The main risk, though, is not from a physical disruption to oil supplies or an oil-producers' embargo which are, as argued in Chapter 1, essentially low-probability occurrences. A greater risk comes from what Paul Horsnell calls a 'fundamental discontinuity' which entails that 'usable excess capacity is eroded away and there is only one mechanism left that can equilibrate the market, and that is a rapid increase in price'.[11] In reality, this was the real reason behind the price rises in the mid-1970s and not the politically-inspired oil embargo which was in practice easily circumvented. At the current time, Middle East OPEC has 60% of known reserves but is producing only 30% of global production from 1% of the world's producing wells. As a consequence, very substantial investment will have to be made in the region if the projected 80% increase in Gulf production over the next ten years is to be realised. Without this investment, there could be sown the conditions for a 'fundamental discontinuity' where excess capacity, currently located almost solely in Saudi Arabia, is eroded.

There is no need to be alarmist about this. There is sufficient capital for such investment and the Gulf OPEC states are inviting back the oil companies to increase production capacity. But, this process can potentially be undermined by the growing anti-Western sentiment in the region, most notably in Saudi Arabia, in response to the 'war on terrorism' after 11 September. In addition, a serious obstacle to promoting a favourable regional investment climate are the Western-imposed sanctions on Iran, Iraq and Libya. These three countries between them have more proven oil reserves than the North Sea, the former Soviet Union and the whole Western Hemisphere combined. Since the Gulf region is such a critical source for Chinese supplies, it is understandable that, from a strictly energy security perspective, China should be greatly exercised by the need to lift these sanctions and permit a favourable investment climate for these countries. One should note, though, that China and other Asian countries have obtained some benefits from the sanctions on these countries. Asian companies, such as China's CNPC and Malaysia's Petronas, have taken the opportunity to penetrate the Iranian and Iraqi markets which would otherwise have been closed to them. This has given them the chance to become genuine global players. However, there is now a clear commercial interest for these companies to see these markets opened so that they can benefit from their investments.

Military and Security Implications

Even if market mechanisms are a critical and sometimes under-rated component of energy security, oil remains a valuable strategic commodity which inevitably promotes a degree of political and military competition between states. The history of the Middle East provides ample evidence of how oil has contributed to conflict and war. In Asia, the impetus for Japanese imperialism was driven in part by Tokyo's perceived need to gain control of key strategic materials, including the oil-fields in Malaysia. The US-imposed embargo on oil and other strategic materials in response to the

Japanese occupation of Manchuria contributed to the Japanese sense of vulnerability and its drive towards expansion. For analysts working within the realist paradigm, the pre-Second World War Japanese analogy is not so distant from the energy dilemmas facing contemporary China. The belief that China is seeking to gain control over its energy arteries – most notably the sea-lines of communication (SLOCs) from the Persian Gulf and over the petroleum reserves in the South and East China Seas – is already exercising military analysts from the region and in the West. In particular, China's naval build-up is viewed as bolstering Beijing's claims over the South and East China Seas and as a response to the need to protect its oil supplies through the Strait of Malacca and beyond.

Even if intuitively attractive, the Japanese imperialist analogy does not match the Chinese situation in one vital detail. Japan's fate has always been to be completely dependent on external energy resources while China possesses, and will continue to possess, significant indigenous resources. In the scenario of a comprehensive embargo, Japan would be militarily paralysed, while China would still have sufficient domestic reserves to ensure that its war-fighting capabilities would not be undermined.[12] Certainly, China's domestic growth and economic development would be greatly damaged by an embargo but this is an inevitable consequence of a war. In general, Japan's energy security is significantly different from China's in that it suffers from a far greater level of dependence on petroleum imports.

It can be argued that presently the comparative levels of energy insecurity are more evenly balanced as Japan is allied to the US while China can justifiably fear scenarios in which the US might seek to hinder or control its energy imports. Yet, the US security umbrella does not completely reassure the Japanese. In particular, China's naval expansion is increasingly viewed as a direct threat to Japan's energy security and this perception is exacerbated by China's territorial claims to the Diaoyu/Senkaku islands in the East China Sea.[13] In April 2000, Japan offered its coast guard forces to lead a regional maritime enforcement operation against piracy in the Strait of Malacca. Indonesia, Malaysia and Singapore all welcomed this initiative with the clear understanding that the main concern was Chinese expansion rather than rising piracy attacks.[14] All these countries have also been enlarging their naval capacities in response to the perceived Chinese threat, which has sparked a regional naval arms race. India has similarly expressed its concerns with Defence Minister George Fernandez arguing in 1998 that India's nuclear capability was required against the Chinese threat, which included, *inter alia*, Chinese naval cooperation with Myanmar and the ambitions of the Chinese navy to expand into the Indian Ocean.[15] As a consequence, the Indian navy is looking towards expanding its activities to the Strait of Malacca and beyond. US military analysts also view the Chinese naval expansion as an important element in the Sino-US strategic competition.[16]

Despite these widespread fears of China's threat to these vital sea-lines, a degree of proportion should be preserved. First, China's naval capabilities have tended to be over-estimated. The delivery from Russia of two *Sovremenny*-class destroyers in 2000 was viewed regionally as a major sign of China's expansionist naval ambitions. In reality, it was an indication of the relative backwardness of Chinese capabilities that the *Sovremennys* were represented as improvements. Although modern by Russian standards, the vessels are a generation behind their American equivalents.[17] Even though the US Pacific Fleet has been reduced in strength by about 40% since 1990, it is still the overwhelming naval power in the region. China's naval expansion has also been compensated, and often over-compensated, by the growth in other regional navies with Taiwan, Japan and South Korea all expanding their submarine and surface fleets. In relative terms, the Indian navy is a much more significant force and is probably one generation ahead of China in terms of capabilities and strategic reach.

Even in the event that China had both the will and the capability to fatally disrupt shipping in the Strait of Malacca and South China Sea, this would not paralyse international shipping. There exist alternative sea-routes to Japan and beyond which would go through the Sunda or Lombok straits and then through the Strait of Makassar. This would result in some increased freightage costs but these would be relatively low. An additional and even more basic problem is that it would be almost impossible for any actor, whether China or the US, to impose an embargo which would discriminate between friends and foe. This is even more the case when international shipping is so globalised, with merchant ships registered in non-involved countries such as Panama and with crews of increasingly indeterminate multinational citizenship. If China were to impede shipping in the South China Sea, it would undoubtedly harm its own supplies. Likewise, if the US were to impose an embargo on China, this would inevitably threaten Japan. There is, therefore, little logic for either side to pursue this path which would ultimately be only self-defeating.

The issues of sealines of communication inevitably becomes entangled with China's expansive territorial claims towards the South and East China seas. It is often claimed that energy considerations have been a critical factor behind China's claims, its diplomatic inflexibility, and the willingness to use force in pursuit of these claims. Certainly, in the East Asian Seas, Chinese petroleum companies have been drilling for oil and gas since the late 1980s and there are fears that their drilling activities might soon encroach on the territorial waters unilaterally claimed by the Japanese government surrounding the Diaoyu/Senkaku islands.[18] It is also true that regional competition over the Spratly Islands in the South China Sea developed quickly once the potential energy resources were identified. There are, though, reasons to doubt whether energy considerations have been foremost in China's strategic thinking. Although nobody knows how much oil is under the Spratly Islands, the best estimate of the Honolulu-based East–West Center is of reserves which could yield production of between 250,000 and 650,000 tonnes per year which would represent less than 0.5% of current Chinese consumption.[19] Chinese policymakers would also be aware that the 20 years of exploration in its off-shore waters, which has also involved $5bn of investment, has resulted in current production of about 20 million tonnes per year, which is less than 10% of China's domestic consumption. Given China's energy needs for the future, the reserves of the South China Sea will do little to resolve China's energy security problems.

It is unlikely, therefore, that energy security has been the key factor behind China's strategic ambitions towards the South and East China Seas. A more plausible reason is a product of what Alastair Iaian Johnston has termed the 'hyper-sovereignty values' which dominate the thinking and behaviour of China's ruling elite which effectively rule out compromise over key territorial and sovereign claims.[20] The historical record also suggests that China has used force primarily in favour of territorial and sovereignty claims rather than for other reasons, such as resource disputes.[21] The Chinese government's willingness to consider joint development zones with other neighbouring states in the South and East China Seas is suggestive that energy resources are not the key geopolitical concern.[22]

Overall, the actual military and security threat to oil supplies tends to be exaggerated. This applies both to Chinese fears as well as the concerns of its neighbours. For the Chinese, even if the US were hypothetically to impose an embargo, it would be extremely difficult to enforce and to ensure that it does not damage the interests of its allies. Such an embargo would not result in China's war-fighting capability being significantly weakened. China, for its part, is far from having the strategic reach to impose significant restrictions to shipping and such restrictions could anyway be by-passed. China is also aware that its vulnerability to disruptions to its vital sea-lanes, particularly with increased dependence on oil imports, is as great if not greater than its potential foes. China's ratification of the third UN Convention of the Law of the Sea in 1996, and its agreement that in principle this should be applied to the South and East China Seas, is an indication of its sense of vulnerability and its interest in safeguarding international norms on freedom of passage.[23]

The role that oil does play, though, is in justifying actions which actually have other rationales. Since oil is so critical to the economies of all these countries, it provides a justification to engage in conflicts which can be easily understood and accepted by politicians and the general public. Military establishments are particularly prone to this. The presumed risk to vital energy supplies, and the competitive struggle for energy resources, is an effective means to justify military and naval build-ups as well as territorial expansion.

Geopolitical Implications for East Asia

Just as energy can be viewed as driving expansionist ambitions in the South and East China Seas, so China's quest for energy sources in Russia and Central Asia can be regarded as promoting broader geopolitical ambitions in East Asia. As has been identified in Chapter 2, the Chinese leadership has been driven by strategic and geopolitical concerns as much as by economic considerations in its 'petroleum diplomacy' towards the energy-rich countries of the former Soviet Union. The impact of this energy diplomacy has been, at least in part, to contribute to the improvement in Sino-Russian relations which has resulted in overcoming decades of intense hostility, the formation of a strategic partnership and the signing of the Friendship and Cooperation Treaty in July 2001. In Central Asia, China's increased involvement has been driven principally by political and strategic concerns. The most visible sign of this diplomatic activism has been the creation of the Shanghai Cooperation Organisation, where Beijing has played a major role in bringing together Russia, China and the Central Asian states into an 'unholy alliance' against Islamist extremism and international terrorism.[24] The desire to build closer relations with Central Asian states has enhanced Beijing's resolve to secure energy supplies from the Caspian region.

The main geopolitical consequence of these developments is that China has secured a quiescent and unthreatening strategic hinterland. This is a remarkable transformation from the mid-1980s when the Soviet Union presented an all-consuming and militarily overwhelming strategic threat. Not only has that threat diminished to near insignificance but the relative balance of power has been radically transformed so that Russia and the Central Asian states have become economically more dependent on the dynamic Chinese market.[25] Russia's willingness to export an array of sophisticated modern weaponry is a clear indication of this.[26] For Chinese strategists and analysts, the main advantage of this transformed hinterland is that diplomatic and military resources can be focused on the more immediate geopolitical challenges to the south, most notably over the Taiwan Straits. Such developments have naturally caused concern for the US and its regional allies as a Sino-Russian *rapprochement* appears to strengthen China's strategic options and provides Beijing with more capabilities to challenge the US-dominated security order in the region.[27]

How much has the energy dimension contributed to this improvement in China's strategic position? In part, it certainly has. The Chinese leadership has not been slow to realise that energy dependence not only creates vulnerabilities; it also provides some foreign policy opportunities. Thus, China's energy market has been used as a carrot to influence countries to adopt policies which are favourable to China's perceived national interests. Beijing's dangling of the prospect of a Central Asian energy linkage resulted in a crackdown on activist Uighur organisations located in the Central Asian states.[28] Interested Western companies have been under similar pressure. For example, Australian businessmen exerted considerable pressure on their government to distance itself from the US over Taiwan so as to improve the chances of winning potential $10bn LNG contracts in China.[29]

Beyond these tactical considerations, energy has also undoubtedly been an important factor in the transformation of relations between China, Russia and Central Asia. For the Central Asian states, the Chinese energy market provides not only an opportunity to break the Russian stranglehold but also a long-term access to a region where continued oil and gas demand is assured. As shown in Chapter 2, Chinese leaders are willing seriously to consider, if not to implement, ambitious and clearly uneconomic pipeline schemes, such as the gas pipeline from Turkmenistan, if they help to project Chinese geopolitical influence into Central Asia. Likewise, the potential development of energy linkages between Russia and China provides a critical economic basis to the relationship which would otherwise be absent. The development of an energy infrastructure between the Russian Far East and China would mean that this peripheral region of Russia would have a greater degree of integration with China and north-east Asia than with distant Moscow. The geopolitical implications of this development would be to further promote China's influence and relative balance of power in Russia's Far East at the expense of the central authorities in Moscow.

The energy factor is therefore certainly a significant factor in strengthening China's geopolitical position in north-east Asia. But, its impact should not be exaggerated. China's influence in Central Asia has been weakened by its decision to postpone construction of the oil pipeline from Kazakhstan and to set aside the idea of a gas pipeline from Turkmenistan. The Central Asian states, in particular those territorially contiguous with China, have not lost their historic distrust of Beijing's intentions and generally prefer Russian tutelage to a Chinese alternative. For its part, China has agreed not to challenge Russia's hegemony in the region, reflecting the fact that Russia and China have broadly congruent geostrategic interests in Central Asia. China is, therefore, being deliberately restrained in its geopolitical penetration into Central Asia and the prospect of a more activist role is only likely when and if plans for oil and gas pipelines from the Central Asian states are more advanced. This appears to be at least a decade away. In the meantime, a more active Chinese role can be envisaged only if Russia were, for some reason or other, to withdraw from the region or if international developments significantly intensify Chinese concerns about energy supplies from the Gulf, such as potentially after the events of 11 September.[30]

Energy considerations have also played a relatively minor role in fostering the warming of relations between Russia and China. Other factors have been more significant, not least the pragmatic resolve of both Chinese and Russian leaders to overcome the debilitating militarised legacy of the Sino-Soviet schism. The defeat of communism in Russia paradoxically provided the foundations for de-escalating the conflict, promoting confidence-building measures between the two countries and for initiating negotiations over outstanding territorial issues. Throughout the 1990s, these pragmatic steps towards normalisation were buttressed by an increasing convergence in Russian and Chinese strategic thinking. Developments such as NATO enlargement and the intervention into Kosovo were seen as dangerous precedents in both Moscow and Beijing. This provided the basis for a common stance on the need to constrain US hegemony, to build a multipolar international order, and to preserve the sanctity of the principle of non-intervention in the internal affairs of states.[31]

Economic factors have certainly played a significant role in giving greater substance to the relationship. As mentioned in

Chapter 2, the trade volumes between Russia and China are as much as ten times lower than trade between China and the US or between China and Japan. Both Russian and Chinese leaders recognise the need to increase the level of trade and notably set themselves an over-ambitious target for $20bn by 2000. Developing the energy resources of Siberia for Chinese markets would certainly consolidate the broader political relationship. But it should be stressed that market considerations will probably dominate over strategic concerns in promoting the integration of Russia's energy infrastructure into north-east Asia. The example of uninterrupted Soviet supply of gas to Western Europe during the Cold War illustrates how energy linkages tend to be relatively autonomous from the broader geopolitical context.

This is not the case, though, for the sale of arms and nuclear technology, which are the more sensitive aspects of contemporary Sino-Russian trade. This trade, unlike energy, is far more dependent on a favourable geopolitical relationship and is also of particular political and socioeconomic importance for both countries. For Russia, China is the largest market for its arms and nuclear industries in a global context where most markets are closed for such Russian exports. For China the Russian arms sales are vital for its military modernisation programme. In strategic terms, these represent the most critical economic transactions in the Sino-Russian strategic relationship. A future energy connection would act primarily to consolidate and entrench the already existing geoeconomic as well as geopolitical relationship.

The assumption that the new-found Sino-Russian *rapprochement* needs to be viewed as threatening to world order or to Western interests can also be reasonably challenged. As a number of analysts have noted, the improvement in relations between Russia and China does not mean that their respective relations to the US and to other Western countries will necessarily become worse or less intense.[32] A number of vital interests of China and Russia, particularly in terms of investment and trade, remain dependent on amicable relations with the West. The dramatic manner in which Russian relations with the US improved after 11 September also illustrates the speed with which Russian strategic priorities can be modified. Some recognition of the contribution that the Sino-Russian relationship has made to improving Asian stability and security should also be given. From conditions of intense militarised conflict, where war was expected to break out at any moment, to the present peaceful and unthreatening conditions, where practically all major territorial and border issues have been resolved, is a significant achievement. Development of a common energy infrastructure would play a prospectively important role in underpinning and consolidating these politico-security gains.

The benefits of such an energy infrastructure would not, though, be limited to just Russia and China. One of the most notable features of the energy map of Asia-Pacific, and particularly north-east Asia, is the clear convergence of interests among the countries of the region. In Asia as a whole, there is a growing dependence on Middle Eastern oil, a common resolve to diversify supplies, and a region-wide environmental drive for cleaner energy which would require a significant shift to the use of gas. This convergence of interests is paralleled by a complementarity in the resources within the region which can be tapped to meet these interests. Abundant energy resources are found in Siberia and in Central Asia and with gas rather than oil probably being in greater supply. However, Russia and the Central Asian states might be resource-rich but they are chronically short of capital to develop these resources. This is in contrast to Japan and South Korea who are capital-rich but almost totally energy deficient and thus could potentially provide investment for developing these energy resources. China, for its part, is both resource deficient and capital poor but has ample labour which could be used for overcoming labour shortages in Siberia and the Russian Far East.[33]

On paper, therefore, there is a clear economic logic for cooperation rather than confrontation over energy developments in north-east Asia. The most ambitious projects, which tend to be for pan-regional gas pipeline grids, reflect this logic.[34] These proposals have hitherto legitimately been considered rather over-optimistic, neglecting the many political and economic obstacles which hinder their realisation. However, China's new-found interest in such cooperation does change the strategic calculus by adding a vast pool of potential new consumers. It also multilateralises the energy equation which tended in the past to focus on bilateral negotiations between the Soviet Union/Russia and Japan and where progress was often vulnerable to the Kuril islands issue. As noted in earlier chapters, consideration is already being given for oil and gas pipelines to provide China with the output from the various projects in Sakhalin. Chinese negotiations with Russia over pipelines between Irkutsk and China are also involving the South Koreans with the potential participation of the Japanese.

The potential for such energy cooperation through building a shared infrastructure is thus a real opportunity for furthering integration in the region. There remain, of course, significant obstacles to such cooperative positive-sum developments, not least the degree of distrust between the major actors in the region. The unresolved territorial and sovereignty issues contribute to the difficulties of building cooperative arrangements. The poor investment climate in the post-Soviet states, and particularly in the Russian Far East, represents a further major obstacle, though improvements have been made in this regard under Putin's administration. For analysts and interested external actors, the most constructive contribution to overcoming these obstacles is through promoting regimes or institutions which can potentially encourage cooperation, facilitate trust, and provide a framework for joint action. It is in this area that Western experience and expertise can perhaps be most helpful in building the transnational energy linkages which are needed in the Asia-Pacific region.

In this regard, it is probably more effective not to be too ambitious and seek to promote an all-encompassing institution or regime for regional energy integration. Rather, there is a need to identify specific and concrete areas where cooperation is desirable and to decide which regime or institution, whether currently existing or not, would be most effective in responding to this need. Following this logic, a number of areas can be identified:

i.   Regional cooperative measures to deal with emergency storage and emergency response plans. China has begun to develop its own strategic reserves but there is no indication of the development of a broader regional capability to resist price-hikes or temporary disruptions to supply.[35] A joint-Asian strategic storage capacity and emergency response plans could also potentially have a direct impact on oil prices. Such arrangements would follow the cooperative measures recommended by the IEA.[36] In the short-term, a north-east Asian grouping, including Japan, Russia, Korea and China would probably be the least problematic. Alternative arrangements could be an ASEAN-based grouping which included China or within the APEC forum.

ii. A regime which included rules on making investments in the energy sector; for the treatment and protection of such investments; and regulations concerning transit issues. The advantage here is that the European Union together with the states of the former Soviet Union have already developed such an instrument, the Energy Charter Treaty, which has been specifically established to deal with these issues for the European and West Asian energy infrastructure.[37] The Treaty could be extended into East Asia and China has already expressed its interest in becoming a signatory.[38] Alternatively, an East Asian energy charter could be developed. The EU could play a potential role in this area.

iii. A regime or institution for promoting a pan-regional gas grid. As mentioned above, it is the creation of such a gas grid which provides potentially the greatest contribution to regional energy integration.[39] In this context, APEC might be the most appropriate forum since it is already studying the development of regional electrical power grids. The UN through the UN Economic and Social Commission for Asia and the Pacific (ESCAP) has also been active in this area. In June 2001, ESCAP organised a North-East Asia Expert Group meeting on Inter-Country Cooperation in Electric Power Sector Development. Consideration at that meeting was also given to the potential of gas trading and pipelines networks.[40] In this context, the gas resources in Russia should be considered in the context of additional gas fields in Malaysia, Indonesia and Alaska.

iv. The encouragement of further joint-development zones to promote the development of petroleum in disputed seas, such as in the South and East China Seas. This could be supplemented by cooperative arrangements on security arrangements for critical sea-lines of communication, such as common policies on maritime piracy. These issues involve sensitive sovereignty concerns, particularly for China, but Beijing has shown an increased willingness to consider such cooperative approaches, particularly in the context of the ASEAN Regional Forum.

This is far from an inclusive list of the potential areas where cooperation on energy-related issues can be of mutual benefit to the countries of the region and where regimes or institutions can play an important role in promoting such cooperation. The European experience might be of some relevance here. The genius of Jean Monnet, the father of European integration, was to focus on the key strategic resources which had traditionally fuelled European wars as the initial basis for integration. Thus, it was the European Coal and Steel Community, which brought these critical war-making resources under supranational control, that became the foundations of the European integration process. Obviously, the European experience is not necessarily applicable to Asia. Pessimists argue that the situation in Asia is closer to late nine-teenth century than post-Second World War Europe.[41] In addition, the cultural and ideological differences and the geographical separation of the countries in Asia are arguably greater than in Europe. Whether this is correct or not, the European example does suggest that a problem-focused multilateral institution or set of regimes might be more productive in generating a process of integration than more ambitious and generalised multilateral forum, such as the ARF or APEC. Such practical problem-driven cooperation might be the best mechanism to promote the functional spillover which has, in the European case at least, been the driving force for economic and political integration.

Implications for Middle East Stability

The dilemma for China is that even if it takes expensive measures to diversify supplies away from the volatile Middle East, fast growing domestic demand will only realistically be satisfied by increased supplies from the Gulf region. Unless China reverts back to a Maoist form of autarchic development, which is almost un-thinkable, China's dependence on Middle East petroleum supplies is destined to grow substantially. It is inevitable, therefore, that China will have important energy-related interests in the Middle East. It will be much more difficult, as was the case during the Gulf war in 1990–1991, for China to adopt a passive posture towards the major conflicts and crises of the region. A key question that this raises is the nature and content of the intensified Chinese engagement in the Middle East. Will it support, or seek to challenge, the position of the US as the principal external security guarantor of the region? More specifically, a significant Western concern is that China might intensify its practice of selling arms to so-called 'rogue' states of the region in exchange for security of energy supplies.[42] This would follow the pattern of Chinese sales of ballistic and cruise missiles and nuclear technology transfers to Iran over the past two decades which have been seen in Washington as the most egregious example of destabilising Chinese behaviour. Do the growing energy needs of China make such arms-for-energy deals even more attractive?

There is undoubtedly a temptation to follow this route to secure oil supplies from the more radical anti-Western oil-exporting states. Shadowy Chinese defence firms continue to import oil from Iran and the US remains legitimately suspicious of Chinese behaviour.[43] However, beyond the particular instances, the clear trend during the 1990s has been for Chinese arms sales generally, and missile and nuclear technology sales in particular, to become increasingly less significant in overall trade terms. From 1990 to 1998, Chinese arms sales declined from $2bn to $500 million in 1998, representing a 75% reduction over the eight-year period.[44] The decline is even more abrupt in the Middle East than in other parts of the developing world. Overall, China's share of the Middle East arms market rest at about 2%, vastly inferior to those of the United States or Russia.[45] The arms market does not, therefore, represent a major economic interest for China, certainly in comparison to its energy interests in the region.

This weak market share is not, though, primarily due to Chinese self-restraint. The most significant factor is the poor quality of Chinese weaponry and the backwardness of Chinese military technology. This is illustrated by the need for China to rely on Russian imports for its own military modernisation programme rather than on its own indigenous capabilities. Other countries will only generally buy Chinese arms if they have absolutely no other possible suppliers. Pakistan, Myanmar and North Korea are countries which fall into this category. Since Iran has now developed a good relationship with Russia, which includes a substantial arms component, there is now little incentive to continue to depend on China.[46]

There remain certain niche areas, such as cruise and ballistic missile sales and nuclear technology transfer, which could still prove attractive to Iran and other Middle Eastern states. However, China has also shown a growing willingness to take a more responsible attitude to such potential sales. This has been partially due to China's gradual acceptance of global arms control and non-proliferation norms, such as the Nuclear Non-Proliferation Treaty (NPT), the Missile Technology Control Regime (MTCR), the Chemical Weapons Convention (CWC) and the Comprehensive Test Ban Treaty (CTBT).[47] It is also closely related to the intensive diplomatic and other pressure that the US has exerted to reduce Chinese incentives towards proliferation.[48] Thus, the United States' conditions for the enactment of the 1985 US-China Peaceful Nuclear Cooperation Agreement was that China institute comprehensive public regulations on nuclear exports and make a specific assurance that it would not provide nuclear-related assistance to Iran.[49] Similar US pressure has been exerted to gain Chinese commitment not to export cruise and ballistic missiles, which resulted in the November 2000 breakthrough when China announced a missile export policy consistent with the MTCR.[50]

US diplomatic pressure has certainly been a critical factor in encouraging Chinese commitment to non-proliferation norms. However, this pressure has probably only been effective since it complemented significant shifts in China's own perceptions of its strategic interests in the Middle East. The example of Iran is illustrative of this. During the Cold War period, Iran was strategically important as a perceived bulwark against Soviet expansionism. In the aftermath of the Tiananmen Square events, Iran was one of the few countries not to join the international diplomatic isolation of China and thus the relationship retained its

significance. During both periods, arms sales represented one of
the key foundations of the Sino-Iranian strategic relationship. The
mid-1990s saw, though, a significant shift in Chinese priorities
towards Iran. There was now no Soviet threat seeking to expand to
the Indian Ocean and China had emerged from its post-Tiananmen
international quarantine. With the loss of energy self-sufficiency,
petroleum diplomacy emerged as the key imperative of Chinese
engagement in the region. As noted in Chapter 2, this diplomacy
had involved outreach beyond China's traditional allies to include
the conservative Gulf countries, such as Saudi Arabia. Sino-Iranian
relations remained important but, from the mid-1990s, the priorities had changed from geopolitics and arms sales to energy economics and petroleum. China's core concern was now to secure
long-term supply contracts with Iran, to promote Chinese investment in Iran, and to encourage Iranian companies themselves to
participate in China's oil industry.[51]

In this changed strategic context, the potentially destabilising
consequences of missile sales to Middle Eastern states, and their
effect on Chinese strategic interests, has become more apparent to
Chinese analysts. The regional impact of the sale of the DF-3
intermediate-range missile to Saudi Arabia appears to have been a
particularly salutary lesson.[52] Chinese analysts and leaders have
regularly declared that strategic stability in the Middle East is a
major policy objective and that China can contribute to such
stability.[53] There is reason to view such declarations as something
more than the routine Chinese propaganda about its peace-loving
intentions. It does reflect a more clearly-defined national interest
that China's energy security, which is becoming increasingly dependent on the Middle East, relies on strategic stability in the
region so as to assure that there are no physical disruptions to
supply. Destabilising arms transfers to the region potentially
undermine this key objective. Chinese divergence with Russian
interests in this regard are illustrative. As a petroleum-exporting
state, Russia does not rely on imports from the region and its own
exports actually benefit from supply disruptions in the Middle
East. There is, therefore, no strictly energy security concerns in
Russia which counter-balance the commercial benefits of its lucra-
tive arms sales to the region. For China, whose arms sales are in

any case minuscule relative to its energy trade, the logic is reversed.

The fact that China has apparently shifted its strategic priorities in the Middle East does not discount the prospect that China will continue to use arms sales as an instrument of influence in the region. Evidence of the proliferation of China's sales to radical countries in the Middle East, most notably Iran, has become such a litmus test of the health of broader Sino-US relations that this issue has assumed a strategic significance disproportionate to its actual impact on Middle Eastern stability. As one analyst has noted, 'China's exports are viewed as an indicator of China's intentions and, specifically, its trustworthiness ... rather than a direct threat to material US national security interests'.[54] This has had a rather perverse consequence that China can itself use the proliferation issue to instrumentalise a more general discontent with US policy. During the EP-3 aircraft crisis in May 2001, a senior, unnamed military official threatened to resume missile sales to Iran and other 'rogue' states in response to the US action.[55] It can, thus, be argued that the broader context of Sino-US relations which will be more significant than energy security concerns in driving continued Chinese proliferation in the region. If anything, energy security considerations should act as a constraining factor on Chinese strategic thinking.

Implications for Domestic Stability

The focus of this chapter has been primarily on the strategic implications of China's energy security policy for Western interests in regional and international security. This is a legitimate concern since China's quest for energy security is transforming China's attitudes, behaviour and geopolitical engagement towards its own neighbourhood, towards Russia and Central Asia and towards the Middle East. There are also implications for global oil supply, for critical sea-lines of communication between the Middle East and China, and for China's territorial claims to the South and East China Seas. The main contention of the argument is that, as an independent variable, China's energy security policy is as likely to promote cooperation and integration than confrontation and challenges to the Western-dominated regional and international order. Clearly, other factors, such as the evolution of the Taiwan issue, could lead China to adopt a more threatening posture, which would change the strategic calculation in relation to energy security policy. On its own, though, it has been argued that the negative strategic consequences of China's drive for energy security should not be exaggerated and that alarmist realist-driven scenarios should be treated with a degree of scepticism.

Whether or not this argument is convincing, it should be stressed that ensuring energy security is not just, or even principally, a question of securing sufficient and undisrupted supplies of energy from abroad to supplement domestic supply. An even more pressing and critical challenge is to ensure the domestic conditions for energy security, which principally involves an effective and successful process of reform and liberalisation of the internal domestic energy market which permits an integration with international energy markets. Even in mature industrialised countries, the failure to manage such internal reforms can have stark energy security consequences. For example, the mistakes in the deregulation of the electricity market in California resulted in disruptions of supply, substantial economic consequences and the perception of a national energy crisis. Similarly, protests against the high levels of taxation on petrol in Western Europe led to supply disruptions which almost brought some countries, most notably the United Kingdom, to the point of an economic breakdown. These events demonstrated that energy security has a very important domestic as well as international dimension.

The challenges that the Chinese leadership faces in promoting such a market-driven internal reform is clearly of a different order of magnitude to those facing mature Western industrial economies. China's energy sector remains defined primarily by the legacy of a centralised command-and-control approach; the framework, structure and reforms required for developing a coherent energy market are poorly understood by Chinese elites; and the incompleteness of many of the institutional and cultural underpinnings of a market economy is compounded by the non-transparent nature of China's political system and its decision-making processes. Energy sector reform will also take place in the context of

China's entry to the WTO, which will place enormous competitive pressures on domestic suppliers. There is also the danger that, as argued in previous chapters, the preference to seek strategic solutions to energy security will continue to be pursued at the expense of a more market-oriented and reformist approach.

The policies required for this market-oriented approach have been described in Chapter 1. They include the need radically to restructure state energy companies alongside the formation of a regulatory framework which ensures competition and minimises monopolistic behaviour and abuse of power. Price liberalisation and other measures to ensure transparency are critical so as to encourage foreign investment and integration with international energy markets. There is also the challenge to ensure the creation of an adequate delivery and distribution infrastructure. A comprehensive energy policy needs also to incorporate strategies towards transport and environment, and generally to introduce substantive measures to constrain demand. As noted in Chapter 1, the Chinese government has to date done little to address these challenges. As was stressed earlier as well, there are many difficulties and many potential pitfalls in implementing such reforms. It is essential that the government proceeds with care.

In recognition of this, three scenarios can be extrapolated from how the government may approach this challenge. The first is that the government simply does nothing and fails to develop a coherent strategy for such market-oriented reforms in the energy sector. The main consequence would be to constrain economic growth, which could have a significant negative knock-on effect on the broader economic reform transition taking place in China. It would also inhibit the development of domestic resources which are primarily located in the non-dynamic, peripheral regions and thereby accentuate the divide between the prosperous coastland and the depressed hinterland. This could have significant consequences for social stability and for the prospects of the 'Develop the West' project. It would also increase the demand for imports and the need to pursue strategic measures for securing these imports, potentially increasing the chances for geopolitical friction. In this context, the realist-informed prognoses for China's future behaviour in its energy diplomacy, which were highlighted above, would be more likely to be realised. The pressure for China to secure greater quantities of supplies from its neighbouring oil 'belt' – Russia, Central Asia and the Middle East – could lead the Chinese leadership to pursue more self-interested, unilateral and potentially aggressive policies. Energy security might not be undermined but it would be gained at a significantly greater cost, both financially and geopolitically.

The second scenario involves the Chinese government introducing an ambitious energy reform strategy which is flawed and results in failure. The possible consequence of this would be a collapse of the national energy systems, especially for electricity, whereby some locations and institutions would have plentiful supply while others would have shortages. If this crisis occurred at a juncture where there were other social or economic tensions, it could result in a major political as well as economic crisis. It would also be a daunting task to rectify the failures of the original reforms and put in place a more effective energy reform strategy. It could potentially undermine the support for economic reforms more generally. The possibility that the government might seek to compensate for these domestic failures with a more assertive and risk-prone foreign policy, which is a common response of authoritarian regimes to domestic challenges to their legitimacy, should also be considered. All these dangers underline the need for such reforms to be introduced carefully and for the government to take as much advice as possible from experts coming from countries where such reforms have been successfully introduced.

The final scenario is the optimistic version where China does formulate a strategy for energy reform and liberalisation and manages to implement it in a systematic manner. This would result, along with adherence to WTO requirements, in China becoming progressively more integrated with international energy markets, reducing the need to pursue strategic measures, and thereby enhancing its security of supply at relatively little cost. Domestically, this would have the benefit of underpinning the wider economic reform programme and promoting the integration of the different regions of China through national electricity grids and a national gas pipeline grid. The benefit that this would have for the internal integration of Chinese society should not be underestimated. In particular, the resulting development of the currently non-dynamic energy-rich regions, such as Xinjiang, would even-out the regional disparities of wealth and thereby promote social stability.

The external strategic implications of this benign scenario are that China would be gradually integrated with global energy markets. This would reduce, though certainly not eliminate, the strategic drive for ensuring security of supply and make the Chinese leadership more confident over energy security concerns. It would also build a strong domestic interest in support of the unimpeded operations of the global energy market. If effectively managed, the reformed state oil companies, like CNPC and Sinopec, could become major players competing with the Western multinationals. Overall, it would strengthen the dynamic process, identified earlier in this chapter, in which energy linkages promote regional and international cooperation and integration rather than confrontation and conflict.

Conclusion

The scale of the challenges facing China as it addresses its present and future energy needs cannot be over-estimated. The fast growth in China's economy since the late 1970s has already meant that China has ceased to be self-sufficient in terms of oil production and has come increasingly to be reliant on foreign imports. The loss of China's 30 years of energy self-sufficiency in the mid-1990s came as a considerable shock to the Chinese leadership. Given China's continuing high rates of economic growth, its vast population and the limits on domestic production, this energy dependence is set to grow at an ever-increasing rate. By 2010, China will become one of the world's major oil importers. Gas consumption is also set to rise as the government seeks to reduce the level of atmospheric pollution arising from the burning of coal. In the broader international context, whether it is in the Middle East, Russia, Central Asia or even Latin America and Africa, China is set to become one of the major players in international energy markets. Overall, the Chinese government faces considerable challenges to ensure that sufficient supplies of oil and gas can be provided at a reasonable cost so that future economic growth can be secured.

The principal aim of this Paper has been to assess the strategic implications of the increasing international role that China will inevitably play in pursuit of its energy needs. Certain features of the 'black box' of China's policy-making process were identified through an analysis of the steps China has already taken in seeking to ensure future energy needs. One such feature, which is a recurrent theme in the paper, is the incomplete and *ad hoc* nature of China's energy policy, which tends to prioritise 'strategic' over 'market' measures to deal with its energy security needs. While the Chinese government has focused most of its attention on strategic measures, such as raising domestic production and in investing in overseas sources of energy, far less effort has been directed to liberalising the internal energy markets and to initiating demand-side measures, such as a coherent transport policy. Strategic measures are an unavoidable and necessary part of energy security, reflecting the strategic nature of oil as a commodity. But, such measures need to be balanced by market-oriented policies which integrate China into international energy markets and ensure a more complete and less expensive energy security policy. It is this need for a more balanced policy which is the main challenge facing Chinese policy makers which, in turn, requires a shift in strategic culture where energy security is seen as much in terms of market mechanisms as state-sponsored geostrategy.

Unfortunately, the current policy-making framework favours actors and interest groups who promote a more strategic than market approach to energy security. As Chapter 2 sought to demonstrate through an analysis of certain key policy decisions in the 1990s, energy policy has increasingly shifted to being a concern of 'high politics' where political and strategic concerns have assumed an equal ranking with economic and commercial considerations. The policymaking process is also notable for its complexity and the multiplicity of actors who bring in a variety of domestic political, military-strategic, commercial and economic interests. The top leadership is also increasingly required to make the final decisions on any large-scale energy projects, particularly those involving foreign countries. What is notably lacking in this process is an actor, such as a ministry of energy or its equivalent, which has a specific mandate to promote a more comprehensive energy policy which includes market-oriented measures. In the absence of such an empowered actor, Chinese state-owned petroleum companies gain an unchecked leverage and influence which permits them to promote their specific commercial interests, in particular their desire to become major international actors and to preserve their domestic monopoly status.

Despite the salience of strategic considerations in Chinese energy policy making, the Chinese government has demonstrated considerable caution over large-scale policies. Although Chinese leaders have often been unrestrained in promising support for grandiose energy projects when meeting foreign leaders, such commitments have frequently been postponed or rejected after an exhaustive process of evaluation has demonstrated their economic inefficiency or their political riskiness. As such, the decisions made by the Chinese government cannot fairly be described as reckless or lacking sufficient consideration. Nevertheless, the government is still willing to implement policies, such as the west-to-east gas pipeline from Xinjiang Province, which will provide supplies more expensive and less economical than those found on international markets. Domestic political and foreign policy concerns can still trump strictly economic and efficiency concerns. The Chinese government has also shown its willingness to flex its strategic muscles in international energy markets, as seen by the aggressive large-scale overseas investments made by Chinese state-owned oil companies.

What are the implications of China's emerging international energy policy for Western strategic interests? Any answer to this question is itself dependent on whether one takes the more general view that China is seeking to challenge and subvert the international *status quo*, as promoted by realist containment theory, or is gradually accommodating itself to the existing international order, as premised on liberal interdependence theory. As set out in Chapter 3, realist-informed and alarming scenarios can plausibly be constructed whereby China's growing presence in international energy markets sustains and entrenches its destabilising and anti-Western behaviour. However, the Paper argues that the prospects for such scenarios would be unlikely to be driven by strictly energy considerations and would be a consequence of a broader break down in Chinese relations with the US and other Western states. As an independent variable, China's needs for foreign energy supplies are more likely to foster interdependence and regional and international integration which should strengthen cooperation and responsible Chinese behaviour. The potential gains in this regard are significant, such as energy linkages in north-east Asia promoting a regional integration process between China and its neighbouring states or a more sustained Chinese commitment to strategic stability in the Middle East as energy imports assume a greater significance over arms exports.

The West can contribute in two ways to ensuring these more benign outcomes in China's evolving energy security policy. First, there is the broader 'grand strategic' context of policy towards China which seeks to engage and integrate China into the international order and where attempts should be made to ensure that conflicts on this higher strategic level do not negatively impact on China's international energy policy making. The second area is the more practical help that Western countries can provide in giving assistance and advice to Chinese policy makers on forming a coherent energy policy which balances strategic energy initiatives with market-driven measures. Western advice and assistance can also be invaluable in promoting structures, regimes and institutions which facilitate regional and international energy cooperation. Instruments like the Energy Charter Treaty, or institutions such as the EU, APEC and the IEA can all usefully encourage cooperation in the energy field. The advantage of such a functionally-oriented focus is that it is a less immediate challenge to China's jealously guarded sovereignty but in practice demands a significant undermining of such sovereign rights so as to secure the benefits to be gained through regional and international integration. In this way, the West can potentially help China both in its integration with the world energy community and its peaceable and unthreatening rise to great power status and responsibility.

Notes

Acknowledgement

The authors gratefully acknowledge the financial support of the Sino-British Fellowship Trust of the British Academy.

Chapter 1

1. United Nations Development Programme, *World Energy Assessment* (New York: UNDP, 2000).
2. Howard Geller, John DeCicco, Skip Laitner and Christopher Dyson, 'Twenty years after the Embargo. US Oil Import Dependence and How it can be Reduced', *Energy Policy* vol. 22, 1994, pp. 471–485; David L. Greene, Donald W. Jones and Paul N. Leiby, 'The Outlook for US Oil Dependency', *Energy Policy* vol. 26, 1998, pp. 55–69; United Nations Development Programme, *World Energy Assessment*.
3. Michael May, *Energy and Security in East Asia* (Stanford, CA: Institute for International Studies, Stanford University, 1998)
4. Paul Horsnell, 'The Probability of Oil Market Disruption: with an emphasis on the Middle East', in *Japanese Energy Security and Changing Global Energy Markets: an Analysis of Northeast Asian Energy Cooperation and Japan's Evolving Leadership Role in the Region*, James Baker III Institute for Public Policy, Rice University, 2000.
5. Horsnell, *ibid.*
6. Horsnell, *ibid.*
7. John H. Lichtblau, 'Oil Imports and National Security: Is There Still a Connection?' *The Energy Journal* vol. 15, Special Issue, 1994, pp. 329–346.
8. May, *Energy and Security in East Asia*.
9. Horsnell, 'The Probability of Oil Market Disruption: with an emphasis on the Middle East'.
10. Ken Koyama, *Japan's Energy Strategies Towards the Middle East*, unpublished PhD Thesis, Centre for Energy, Petroleum and Mineral Law and Policy, University of Dundee, 2001; Tsutomu Toichi and Masahisa Naitoh, 'Japan's Energy Security and Petroleum Policies', *Oxford Energy Forum*, May 2001, pp. 3–4; Lindsay Fairhead and Karen Schneider, 'Do Economic Policy and Energy Security in Japan have complementary or Competing Objectives?', *Oxford Energy Forum*, May 2001, pp. 5–7.
11. John Mitchell, *The New Economy of Oil. Impacts on Business, Geopolitics and Society* (London: Earthscan, 2001).

[12] Edward L. Morse and Amy Myers Jaffe, *Strategic Energy Policy Challenges for the 21st Century*, James Baker III Institute for Public Policy, Rice University, 2001; National Energy Policy Development Group, *National Energy Policy. Reliable, Affordable, and Environmentally Sound Energy for America's Future* (Washington, DC: US Government, 2001); Asia Pacific Energy Research Centre, *Emergency Oil Stocks and Energy Security in the APEC Region* (Tokyo: Asia Pacific Energy Research Centre, 2000); European Commission, *Green Paper. Towards a European Strategy for the Security of Energy Supply* (Luxembourg: European Communities, 2001).

[13] Darwin C. Hall, 'Oil and National Security', *Energy Policy* vol. 20, 1992, pp. 1089–1096; European Commission, *Green Paper. Towards a European Strategy for the Security of Energy Supply*; Michael Lynch, 'Oil Scarcity, Energy Security and Long-Term Oil Prices – Lessons Learned (and Unlearned)', *International Association for Energy Economics, Newsletter* First Quarter 1999, pp. 4–8; Asia Pacific Energy Research Centre, *Emergency Oil Stocks and Energy Security in the APEC Region*; National Energy Policy Development Group, *National Energy Policy. Reliable, Affordable, and Environmentally Sound Energy for America's Future*; R. Belgrave, C.K. Ebinger and H. Okino, *Energy Security to 2000*, (Aldershot: Gower, 1987); United Nations Development Programme, *World Energy Assessment*; Geller, Laitner and Dyson, 'Twenty Years After the Embargo. US Oil Import Dependence and How it can be Reduced'; George C. Georgiou, 'US Energy Security and Policy Options for the 1990s', *Energy Policy* vol. 21, 1993, pp. 831–839; International Energy Agency, *Oil Supply Security. The Emergency Response Potential of IEA Countries in 2000* (Paris: OECD/IEA, 2001).

[14] For example location and nature of the stocks, and ownership and operational control. See Asia Pacific Energy Research Centre, *Emergency Oil Stocks and Energy Security in the APEC Region*.

[15] Commercial energy refers to energy traded on commercial markets. This would therefore include nearly all forms of oil, natural gas, coal and electricity, but would normally exclude biomass.

[16] Jonathan Sinton and David Fridley, 'What Goes Up: Recent trends in China's Energy Consumption', *Energy Policy* vol. 28, 2000, pp. 671–687.

[17] Sinton and Fridley, *ibid.*

[18] Sinton and Fridley *ibid.*

[19] Sinton and Fridley, *ibid.*

[20] *BP Statistical Review of World Energy*, various years (London: British Petroleum).

[21] Kenneth B. Medlock and Ronald Soligo, 'The Composition and Growth of Energy Demand in China', in *China and Long-Range Asia Energy Security: An Analysis of the Political, Economic and Technological Factors*, James Baker III Institute for Public Policy, Rice University, 1999; International Energy Agency, *World Energy Outlook 2000* (Paris: OECD/IEA, 2000); British Petroleum, *BP Statistical Review of World Energy 2001* (London: British Petroleum, 2001); Wenrui Jia et al., *The Development Strategy for China's Oil Industry, 1996–2010* (Beijing: Petroleum Industry Press, 1999, in Chinese); Fengqi Zhou and Dadi Zhou, *Medium and Long Term Energy Strategies for China* (Beijing: China Planning Publishing House, 1999 in Chinese).

[22] Kang Wu, *Fossil Energy Consumption and Supply Security in*

Northeast Asia. Policy Paper 36 (La Jolla, CA: University of California Institute on Global Conflict and Cooperation, 1998). Zhou and Zhou, *Medium and Long Term Energy Strategies for China*.

23   International Energy Agency, *World Energy Outlook 2000*. Medlock and Soligo, 'The Composition and Growth of Energy Demand in China'.

24   Medlock and Soligo, 'The Composition and Growth of Energy Demand in China'; International Energy Agency, *World Energy Outlook 2000*; Jia et al., *The Development Strategy for China's Oil Industry, 1996–2010*; Zhou and Zhou, *Medium and Long term Energy Strategies for China*; Jiacheng Wang, 'Oil Demand and Substitution Strategy in China', *China's Industrial Economy*, no. 3, 2000, pp. 38–41 (in Chinese); Baoheng Shi et al. (eds), *Energy Resources and Sustainable Development* (Beijing: China Science and Technology Press, 1999, in Chinese); Shixian Gao, 'China', in Paul B. Stares (ed.) *Rethinking Energy Security in Asia* (Tokyo: Japan Center for International Exchange, 2000), pp. 43–58; Erica Strecker Downs, *China's Quest for Energy Security*, RAND Report MR-1244-AF, 2000; Anthony H. Cordesman, *The Changing Geopolitics of Energy – Part VI. Regional Developments in East Asia, China and India*. (Washington DC: Center for Strategic and International Studies, 1998).

25   Institute of Quantitative and Technical Economics, *Electrical Power Development and the Nuclear Energy Option in China* (Beijing: Chinese Academy of Social Sciences, 2000, in Chinese).

26   Zhou and Zhou, *Medium and Long Term Energy Strategies for China*.

27   Medlock and Soligo, 'The Composition and Growth of Energy Demand in China'; International Energy Agency, *World Energy Outlook 2000*; British Petroleum, *BP Statistical Review of World Energy 2001*; Jia et al., *The Development Strategy for China's Oil Industry, 1996–2010*; Zhou and Zhou, *Medium and Long term Energy Strategies for China*; Jijiang Zhang and Yi Wang, 'The Non-Nuclear Subsitution Option. Strategic Adjustment of China's Energy Structure', *Strategy and Management*, no.4, 1998, pp. 91–97 (in Chinese); Gao, 'China'; Downs, *China's Quest for Energy Security*. Cordesman, *The Changing Geopolitics of Energy – Part VI. Regional Developments in East Asia, China and India*; Fereidun Fesharaki, Sara Banaszak and Kang Wu, *The Outlook for Energy Supply and Demand in Northeast Asia*, University of California Institute on Global Conflict and Cooperation, Policy Paper 36, 1998; Energy Research Institute, *Role of Natural Gas in China's Energy Economy and Gas Demand/ Supply Outlook to 2010/2020*, IEA-China Conference on Natural Gas Industry, 9–10 November 1999, Beijing; Xiaojie Xu, *The Gas Dragon's Rise; Chinese Natural Gas Strategy and Import Patterns*, IEA-China Conference on Natural Gas Industry, 9–10 November 1999, Beijing; Keun-Wook Paik, *Transnational Pipeline Gas Introduction and its Implications Towards China's Gas Expansion*, IEA-China Conference on Natural Gas Industry, 9–10 November 1999, Beijing; Jinzhong Jia, 'Preliminary Discussion on the Development and Utilisation of Natural Gas in the West of China, and its Counter-Measures', *China Energy* no. 7, 2000, pp. 7–10 (in Chinese).

28   Xuchao Yan and Jingmin Yang, *Fuelling China in the Twenty-First Century. A Report to Raise the*

International Competitiveness of China's Oil Industry (Beijing: Enterprise Management Press, 1999, in Chinese); Fengqi Zhou, 'Challenges Facing the Energy Industry of China in the Twenty-First Century', *China Energy* vol.12, no.3, 1999, pp. 3–6 (in Chinese); Lianzhong Li and Liandi Li, 'On Developing China's Large Transnational Oil Corporations', *China's Industrial Economy*, no.2, 2000, pp. 44–48 (in Chinese); Huai Chen, 'China's Oil Security Strategy should be Based on "Going Out" ', *Review of Economic Research* , vol. 25, 2001, pp. 2–5 (in Chinese).

29 International Energy Agency, *China's Worldwide Quest for Energy Security* (Paris: OECD/IEA, 2000).

30 Ronald Soligo and Amy Jaffe, 'China's Growing Energy Dependence: The Costs and Policy Implications of Supply Dependence', in *China and Long-Range Asia Energy Security: An Analysis of the Political, Economic and Technological Factors*, James Baker III Institute for Public Policy, Rice University, 1999.

31 FACTS Inc., 'China Accelerates Shift in Energy Policy, Restructuring of State Petroleum Firms', *Oil and Gas Journal*, January 10, 2000, pp. 14–18.

32 *Asian Energy News*, February 2000, p. 3.

33 British Petroleum, *BP Statistical Review of World Energy 2001*. Xiaojie Xu, 'The Gas Dragon's Rise: Chinese Natural Gas Strategy and Import Patterns', in *China and Long-Range Asia Energy Security: An Analysis of the Political, Economic and Technological Factors*, James Baker III Institute for Public Policy, Rice University, 1999; Zhou, *Role of Gas in China's Energy Economy and Long-Term Forecast for Natural Gas Demand*; US Energy Information

Administration, *China Country Analysis Brief, April 2001*, www.eia.doe.gov. Xinshan Zhu and Wucheng Song, 'Strategic Significance of Developing and Exploiting Methane: Importance, Necessity and Urgency', *China Energy* no. 10, 2000, pp. 8–12 (in Chinese).

34 Medlock and Soligo, 'The Composition and Growth of Energy Demand in China'; International Energy Agency, *World Energy Outlook 2000*; British Petroleum, *BP Statistical Review of World Energy 2001*; Jia et al., *The Development Strategy for China's Oil Industry, 1996–2010*; Zhou and Zhou, *Medium and Long-term Energy Strategies for China*; Wang, 'Oil Demand and Substitution Strategy in China'; Shi et al., *Energy Resources and Sustainable Development*. Gao, 'China'; Downs, *China's Quest for Energy Security*; Cordesman, *The Changing Geopolitics of Energy – Part VI. Regional Developments in East Asia, China and India*; Asia Pacific Energy Research Centre, *Emergency Oil Stocks and Energy Security in the APEC Region*; Wang, 'Oil Demand and Substitution Strategy in China'.

35 British Petroleum, *BP Statistical Review of World Energy 2001*.

36 A sour crude oil is one with a high content of sulphur which increases the corrosive effect of the oil on metals. Refineries which are to be fed with sour crude oil have to be constructed with higher-grade materials than normal crude oil.

37 Philip Andrews-Speed, 'The Challenges Facing China's Gas Industry', *LNG Journal* May/June 2001, pp. 26–29.

38 British Petroleum, *BP Statistical Review of World Energy 2001*; Jia et al., *The Development Strategy for China's Oil Industry, 1996–2010*; Zhou and Zhou, *Medium and*

Long-term Energy Strategies for China; Zhang and Wang, 'The Non-Nuclear Substitution Option. Strategic Adjustment of China's Energy Structure'; Gao, 'China'; Downs, *China's Quest for Energy Security*; Cordesman, *The Changing Geopolitics of Energy – Part VI. Regional Developments in East Asia, China and India*; Fesharaki, Banaszak and Wu, *The Outlook for Energy Supply and Demand in Northeast Asia*; Energy Research Institute, *Role of Natural Gas in China's Energy Economy and Gas Demand/Supply Outlook to 2010/2020*; Paik, *Transnational Pipeline Gas Introduction and its Implications Towards China's Gas Expansion*; Jia, 'Preliminary Discussion on the Development and Utilisation of Natural Gas in the West of China, and its Counter-Measures'. Zhang and Wang, 'The Non-Nuclear Substitution Option. Strategic Adjustment of China's Energy Structure'. 'The Great Perspective on the Methane Industry in China', http://www.cei.gov.cn/, July 2000.

39 Medlock and Soligo, 'The Composition and Growth of Energy Demand in China'; International Energy Agency, *World Energy Outlook 2000*. British Petroleum, *BP Statistical Review of World Energy 2001*; Jia et al., *The Development Strategy for China's Oil Industry, 1996–2010*; Zhou and Zhou, *Medium and Long Term Energy Strategies for China*; Wang, 'Oil Demand and Substitution Strategy in China'; Shi et al., *Energy Resources and Sustainable Development*; Gao, 'China'; Downs, *China's Quest for Energy Security*; Cordesman, *The Changing Geopolitics of Energy – Part VI. Regional Developments in East Asia, China and India*; Asia Pacific Energy Research Centre,

Emergency Oil Stocks and Energy Security in the APEC Region; Wang, 'Oil Demand and Substitution Strategy in China'; Center for Strategic and International Studies, *The Geopolitics of Energy in Asia*, (Washington DC: Center for Strategic and International Studies, 1999). Asia-Pacific Center for Security Studies, *Energy Security in the Asia-Pacific: Competition or Cooperation?* Asia-Pacific Center for Security Studies, Seminar Report, 15 January 1999. Fesharaki, Banaszak and Wu, *The Outlook for Energy Supply and Demand in Northeast Asia*.

40 Coal International Advisory Board, *Coal in the Energy Supply of China* (Paris: OECD/IEA, 1999).

41 Downs, *China's Quest for Energy Security*; Paik, *Transnational Pipeline Gas Introduction and its Implications Towards China's Gas Expansion*; Zhou, *Role of Gas in China's Energy Economy and Long-Term Forecast for Natural Gas Demand*; Zhang and Wang, 'The Non-Nuclear Substitution Option. Strategic Adjustment of China's Energy Structure'.

42 State Planning Commission, '95 *Energy Report of China*. Feng Ai, 'An Analysis of the Oil Problem and Related Policies', *Strategy and Management*, no. 6, 1995, pp. 103–111 (in Chinese). Zhen Zhang, 'Ten Major Steps Necessary for the Development of China's refining Industry in the Twenty-First Century', *International Petroleum Economics*, vol.8, no.1, 2000, pp. 37–39 (in Chinese).

43 British Petroleum, *BP Statistical Review of World Energy 2001*.

44 Jia et al., *The Development Strategy for China's Oil Industry, 1996–2010*.

45 Keun-Wook Paik, *Gas and Oil in Northeast Asia. Policies, Projects and*

Prospects (London: Royal Institute of International Affairs, 1995).

46 *FSU Oil and Gas Monitor* 24 July 2001, pp. 12–13.

47 Main sources: *China Economic Review*, July 1998, p. 8; Downs, *China's Quest for Energy Security.*

48 State Power Corporation, *Electric Power Industry in China 1999*, (Beijing: China Electric Power Information Center, 1999).

49 See, for example, 'China: Crude Imports Surge as Refineries Hit Record Runs', *Weekly Petroleum Argos*, 9 September 1996, p. 4.

50 British Petroleum, *BP Statistical Review of World Energy*, various years.

51 British Petroleum, *ibid*.

52 'High Oil Prices Fuel Delay of State's Tax Adjustment', *China Daily Business Weekly* 20–26 August 2000, p. 3.

53 Zhou, 'Challenges Facing the Energy Industry of China in the Twenty-First Century'.

54 Hong Ma and Zhu Sun, 'Political Thoughts on Establishing China's Strategic Oil Stock', *Strategy and Management* no. 1, 1997, pp. 46–51 (in Chinese). Yan and Yang, *Fuelling China in the Twenty-First Century. A Report to Raise the International Competitiveness of China's Oil Industry.*

55 APERC estimated that the state oil companies held stocks of about 40 million tonnes in 1997 (Asia Pacific Energy Research Centre, *Emergency Oil Stocks and Energy Security in the APEC Region*), and Yan Xuachao and Yang Jingming, (China's Oil Industry in the Twenty-First century) estimated a total of about 60 million tonnes of storage for 1998.

56 'Sounder Oil Reserve System', *China Daily Hong Kong Edition*, 29 June 2001, http://www.chinadaily.com.cn/; 'China's Oil. Taken Hostage', *The*

Economist, 14 July 2001, pp. 64–65; Jia, 'Preliminary Discussion on the Development and Utilisation of Natural Gas in the West of China, and its Counter-Measures'.

57 Yan and Yang, *Fuelling China in the Twenty-First Century. A Report to Raise the International Competitiveness of China's Oil Industry.*

58 'China to Build Underground Natural Gas Storage Area' China Online 2 November 1999, http://www.chinaonline.com/industry/energy/.

59 Yongkun Qian and Ping Jian, 'Issues and Countermeasures of China's Energy Industry after Entry to WTO', *China Energy* no. 1. 2000, pp. 5–8 (in Chinese); Chen, 'Development and Reform of China's Petroleum Industry in the Early Twenty-First Century'.

60 Philip Andrews-Speed, Stephen Dow and Zhiguo Gao, 'An Evaluation of the Ongoing Reforms to China's Government and State Sector: the Case of the Energy Industry', *Journal of Contemporary China* vol. 9, no. 23, 2000, pp. 5–20.

61 Philip Andrews-Speed and Stephen Dow, 'Reform of China's Electric Power Industry. Challenges Facing the Government,' *Energy Policy* vol. 28, 2000, pp. 335–347; Philip Andrews-Speed, Stephen Dow and Minying Yang, 'Regulating Energy in Federal Transition Economies: the Case of China, in Gordon MacKerron and Peter Pearson (eds) *The International Energy Experience. Markets, Regulation and Environment* (London: Imperial College Press, 2000), pp. 91–102.

62 Robert A. Manning, *The Asian Energy Factor. Myths and Dilemmas of Energy Security, and the Pacific Future* (New York: Palgrave, 2000).

63 Philip Andrews-Speed, 'China's

Energy Policy in Transition: Pressures and Constraints', *Journal of Energy Literature* vol. 7, no. 2, 1999, pp. 3–34.

Chapter 2

1 Interview in Beijing, November 2000.
2 See, for instance, David M. Lampton (ed.), *Policy Implementation in Post-Mao China*, (Berkeley: University of California Press, 1987); and Thomas W. Robinson and David Shambaugh (eds), *Chinese Foreign Policy: Theory and Practice* (Oxford: Clarendon Press, 1996).
3 Kenneth G. Lieberthal and Michel Oksenberg, *Bureaucratic Politics and Chinese Energy Development*, (Washington, DC: Government Printing Office, 1986), p. 137.
4 Kenneth G. Lieberthal, *Governing China: From Revolution through Reform*, (New York: W. W. Norton, 1995), pp. 158–61. James C. F. Wang, *Contemporary Chinese Politics: An Introduction*, Sixth Edition (New Jersey: Prentice Hall, 1999), p. 97.
5 Kenneth G. Lieberthal and Michel Oksenberg, *Policy Making in China: Leaders, Structures and Processes* (Princeton University Press, 1998), p. 30.
6 Li Cheng, 'China in 2000: A Year of Strategic Rethinking', *Asian Survey*, vol. 41, no. 1, January/February 2001.
7 The White Paper for the first time indicated that an indefinite refusal to negotiate by the authorities on Taiwan (and not just an explicit declaration of independence) could prompt China to take military action. For the text, see *White Paper: The one-China principle and the Taiwan question* (Beijing: Taiwan Affairs Office & Information Office of the State Council, 21 February 2000). For a

fuller discussion, see Avery Goldstein, 'The Diplomatic Face of China's Grand Strategy: A Rising Power's Emerging Choice', *China Quarterly*, No. 168, December 2001, pp. 835–864.
8 *Beijing Review*, 10 April 2000. The policy was issued by the Chinese government at the Ninth National People's Congress in March 2000.
9 *People's Daily*, 26 February 2000.
10 Cheng, 'China in 2000', p. 85.
11 For a detailed discussion of the new generation, see Li Cheng, *China's Leaders: The New Generation* (Lanham: Rowman & Littlefields, 2001).
12 See, Michael Swaine, *The Role of the Chinese Military in National Security Policymaking* (Santa Monica, CA: RAND, 1997).
13 Greg Austin, *China's Ocean Frontier: International Law, Military Force and National Development* (Sydney: Allen and Unwin, 1998), p. 313. The relevant legislation passed in February 1992 was entitled the 'Law of the People's Republic of China on its Territorial Waters and their Contiguous Areas'.
14 Mehmet Ogutcu, 'China's Energy Future and Global Implications' in Werner Draghun and Robert Ash (eds), *China's Economic Security* (New York: St Martin's Press, 1999), pp. 84–141.
15 Philip Andrews-Speed, *et al.* 'The ongoing reforms to China's government and state sector: the case of the energy industry', *Journal of Contemporary China*, vol. 23, No. 9, 2000; pp. 12–13; see also Fereidun Fesharaki and Kang Wu, 'Revitalizing China's Petroleum Industry through Reorganization: Will it Work? *Oil and Gas Journal*, 10 August 1998.
16 Andrews-Speed, *et al.* 'The ongoing reforms to China's government and state sector: the case of the energy industry', p. 9.

17 *CNPC Yearbook, 1999* (Beijing: Oil Industry Press, 1999) pp. 56–59.

18 Andrews-Speed, 'The ongoing reforms to China's government and state sector: the case of the energy industry', pp. 12–13.

19 *CNPC Yearbook, 2000* (Beijing: Oil Industry Press, 2000), pp. 58–59.

20 Andrews-Speed, 'The ongoing reforms to China's government and state sector: the case of the energy industry', p. 12.

21 *CNPC Yearbook 1999*, p. 38.

22 Ma Fucai (CNPC president), 'Report at CNPC working conference', 19 January 1999, in *CNPC Yearbook 2000*, pp. 34–45.

23 'Vice-Premier Wu Bangguo inspects Daqing oil field and Daqing petrochemical plant', 4 August 1999, in *CNPC Yearbook 1999*, pp. 59–60.

24 Ma Fucai, 'Speeches at opening of the conference attended by senior CNPC officials', 7 June 1999, in *CNPC Yearbook 2000*, pp. 46–51.

25 See, Peter Cheung and James Tang, 'The external relations of China's provinces', in D. M. Lampton (ed.), *The Making of Chinese Foreign and Security Policy in the Era of Reform, 1978–2000*, (Stanford, CA: Stanford University Press, 2001), pp. 91–120.

26 See, Xuanli Liao, *Chinese Think-Tanks and China's Japan Policy*, PhD dissertation, University of Hong Kong, 2002.

27 *History of the Petroleum Industry*, (Urumqi: Xinjiang People's Press, 1999, in Chinese), pp. 39–45.

28 'China's Leaders Throw Their Weight behind West-East Gas Pipeline', *Gas Matters*, October 2000, pp. 3–4.

29 *Ibid.*, p. 6.

30 For a good overview of recent development in Xinjiang, see Nicolas Becquelin, 'Xinjiang in the Nineties', *The China Journal*, no. 44, July 2000. See also John Calabrese, 'China's Policy towards Central Asia: Renewal and Accommodation', *Eurasian Studies*, No. 16, Autumn–Winter, 1999.

31 David Shambaugh, 'China's Ambivalent Diplomacy', *Far Eastern Economic Review*, 15 November 2001.

32 'China's rebellious province', *The Economist*, 23 August 1997.

33 For the Chinese reactions, see 'Rapid-reaction units "needed in separatist battle" ', *South China Morning Post*, 18 January 2002; and 'Xinjiang separatists linked to bin Laden', *South China Morning Post*, 21 January 2002.

34 'China's "Go West" Program Threatened', *Stratfor.com*, 6 November 2000.

35 Susan V. Lawrence, 'Where Beijing Fears Kosovo', *Far Eastern Economic Review*, 7 September 2000.

36 'Jiang says Helping Poor Key to Stability', *South China Morning Post*, 5 February 2002.

37 According to one investment bank – Salomon Smith Barney – the first five years of China joining the WTO will result in 40m people losing their jobs, as reported in *Far Eastern Economic Review*, 5 October 2000.

38 *People's Daily*, 29 April 1994.

39 Ouan Lan and Keun-Wook Paik, *China Natural Gas Report* (London: Royal Institute of International Affairs, 1998), pp. 112–3.

40 Interview with Chinese specialists in Beijing in November 2000.

41 Philip Andrews-Speed and Sergei Vinogradov, 'China's Involvement in Central Asian Petroleum: Convergent or Divergent Interests?', *Asian Survey*, vol. 45, no. 2, March/April 2000, p. 392–3.

42 *Petroleum Intelligence Weekly*, 29 September 1997, pp. 1–2. See also Erica Strecker Downs, *China's Quest for Energy Security* (St Monica, CA: RAND, 2000), pp. 15–6.

43 'Aktobemunaygas Employees fed up with CNPC Management, *Kazakhstan: Oil and Gas Update*, January 2000.

44 Gregory Gleason, 'Policy Dimensions of West Asian Borders after the Shanghai Accord', *Asian Perspective*, vol. 25, no. 1, 2001, pp. 107–31.

45 Jean-Christophe Peuch, 'Central Asia: Uighurs say States Yield to Chinese Pressure', *Radio Free Europe/Radio Liberty*, 29 March 2001.

46 Shiping Tang, 'Economic Integration in Central Asia: The Russian and Chinese Relationship', *Asian Survey*, vol. 40, no. 2, March/April 2000, p. 367–8.

47 For the most extensive analysis of Sino-Russian relations, see Sherman Garnett (ed.), 'Limited Partnership. Russian-Chinese Relations in a Changing Asia', (Washington, DC: Brookings Institution Press, 1998). See also Gilbert Rozman, 'Sino-Russian relations in the 1990s: a balance sheet', *Post-Soviet Affairs*, vol. 14, no. 2, 1998; Jennifer Andersen, *'The Limits of Sino-Russian Strategic Partnership'*, Adelphi Paper, no. 315 (Oxford: Oxford University Press, 1998); Rajan Menon, 'The Strategic Convergence Between Russia and China', *Survival*, vol. 39, no. 2, 1997.

48 *Chinese Statistics Yearbook, 2001* (Beijing: Chinese Statistics Press, 2001).

49 Yu Bin, 'Putin's Ostpolitik and Sino-Russia Relations', *Comparative Connections*, October 2000, p. 5.

50 Philip Andrews-Speed, 'Natural Gas in East Siberia and the Russian Far East: A View from the Chinese Corner', *Cambridge Review of International Affairs*, vol. 12, no. 1, Summer/Fall 1998; and Keun-Wook Paik, 'Sino-Russia Oil and Gas Development

Cooperation: The Reality and the Implications', *Journal of Energy and Development*, vol. 22, no. 2, 1998.

51 Eugene Khartukov, 'Prospects for Russian gas supply to East Asia', *FT Asia Gas Report*, May 1999.

52 Ogutcu, 'China's Energy Future and Global Implications', p. 95.

53 'China Eyes Foreign Investors for Shanghai Gas Grid', *Reuters*, 29 January 2002.

54 Micheal Lelyveld, 'Russia: Moscow Promises Energy Exports to China', *Radio Free Europe/Radio Liberty*, 19 July 2001; and FSU *Oil & Gas Monitor*, 24 July 2001, p. 12.

55 Dongfang Xiao, 'China and the EU: Seeking strategic cooperation in the Middle East region', *Western Asia and Africa* (in Chinese), 1999, no. 6, p. 13.

56 Hashim Behehani, *China's Foreign Policy in the Arab World* (London: Routledge, 1985).

57 Yang Guang, 'China's Stabilising Role', in John Calabrese (ed.), *Gulf-Asia Energy Security* (Washington, DC: Middle East Institute, 1998).

58 For a fuller analysis, see John Calabrese, 'China and the Persian Gulf: Energy and Security', *Middle East Journal*, vol. 52, no. 3, Summer 1998, pp. 351–66.

59 *China Oil, Gas and Petrochemicals*, vol. 21, no. 7, pp. 11–12. Yitzhak Shichor, 'China's economic relations with the Middle East: new dimensions,' *China Report*, vol. 34, no. 3 & 4, 1998.

60 Xiaojie Xu, 'China and the Middle East: Cross-Investment in the Energy Sector', *Middle East Policy Council*, vol. 7, no. 3, June 2000.

61 'China Leaps on to Global Oil Production Stage', *Petroleum Intelligence* Weekly, 9 June 1997 and *China Daily*, 6 June 1997.

62 Hassan Hadifh, 'Iraq and China Sign $1.2bn Oil Contract', *Reuters*, 4 June 1997.

63 Xu, 'China and the Middle East',

pp. 7–8; *1997 Middle East Economic Survey*, vol. 40, no. 24, 16 June 1997; *China Oil, Gas and Petrochemicals*, vol. 21, no. 7, pp. 11–12.

64 Wang Jinglie, 'Strategic Position of the Middle East and Adjustment of the US Middle East Policy', *Western Asia and Africa* (in Chinese), no. 2, 1998, pp. 58–9.

Chapter 3

1 Ken Koyama, *Japan's Energy Strategies Towards the Middle East*, unpublished PhD Thesis, Centre for Energy, Petroleum and Mineral Law and Policy, University of Dundee, 2001.

2 For a general overview of the debate, see Denny Roy, 'The "China Threat" Issue: Major Arguments', *Asian Survey*, vol. 37, no. 8, August 1996, pp. 758–81. See also Richard Bernstein and Ross H. Munro, 'China I: The Coming Conflict with China', *Foreign Affairs*, vol. 76, no. 2, March/April 1997, pp. 12–22; Gerald Segal, 'East Asia and the Constrainment of China', *International Security*, vol. 20, no. 4, Spring 1996, pp. 107–35; Gideon Rachman, 'Containing China', *Washington Quarterly*, vol. 19, no. 1, Winter 1996, pp. 129–40; and Michael E. Brown, Owen R Coté, Jr., Sean M. Lynn-Jones and Steven E. Miller (eds), *The Rise of China: An International Security Reader* (Cambridge, MA: The MIT Press, 2000).

3 The main exponent of the more pessimistic view is Kent E. Calder, *Asia's Deadly Triangle: How Arms, Energy and Growth Threaten to Destabilise Asia-Pacific* (London: Nicholas Brealy Publishing, 1996). See also Mamdouh G. Salameh, 'China Oil and the Risks of Regional Conflict', *Survival*, vol. 37, no. 4, Winter 1995–6.

4 Keun-Wook Paik, *Gas and Oil in Northeast Asia: Policies, Projects and Prospects* (London: Royal Institute of International Affairs, 1995), pp. 261–74.

5 'The Influence of Asia on Oil Price Fluctuations', *Alexander's Oil and Gas Connections: News and Trends: S and SE Asia*, vol. 6, no. 15, 14 August 2001.

6 For an extended discussion, see Fereidun Fesharaki and Kang Wu, *Outlook for Energy Demand, Supply and Government Policies in China* (Honolulu, HI: East-West Center, 29 August 1998).

7 See, for example, Vaclav Smil, 'The Energy Question Again', *Current History*, December 2000, pp. 408–12; and Colin Campbell, *The Coming Oil Crisis* (Brentwood: Multi-Science Publishing, 1997).

8 Robert A. Manning, *The Asian Energy factor: Myths and Dilemmas of Energy Security, and the Pacific Future* (New York: Palgrave, 2000).

9 For arguments on how the markets provide for energy security, see Dennis O'Brien, 'Mightier than the Sword: Energy Markets and Global Security', *Harvard International Review*, vol 19, no. 3, Summer 1997, pp. 8–11, 62–63; Fereidun Fesharaki, 'Oil Markets and Security in Northeast Asia', *Policy Paper 35*, University of California Institute on Global Conflict and Cooperation, pp. 23–5; and Daniel Yergin, Dennis Eklof and Jefferson Edwards, 'Fueling Asia's Recovery', *Foreign Affairs*, vol. 77, no. 2, March/April 1998, pp. 34–50.

10 Quoted in Norman Selley, 'Changing Oil', *RIIA Briefing Paper*, no. 10, January 2000, p. 3. See also Michael C. Lynch, 'Oil Scarcity, Energy Security and Long-Term Oil Prices – Lessons Learned (and Unlearned), *IAEE Newsletter*, First Quarter 1999.

11 Paul Horsnell, 'The Probability of Oil Market Disruption: With an Emphasis on the Middle East' in www.bakerinstitute.org.

12 Michael May, 'Energy and Security in East Asia', *Asia-Pacific Research Center Working Paper*, January 1998.

13 'Energy Security revisited (1): Japanese Fears and IEA Concerns', *Energy Economist*, no. 235, May 2001, pp. 3–7; and 'Japan wary of Assertive China', *Janes's Intelligence Review*, December 2000. For an analysis of the Diaoyu/Senkaku islands issue, see Unryu Suganama, *Sovereign Rights and Territorial Space in Sino-Japanese Relations: Irredentism and the Diaoyu/Senkaku Islands* (Honolulu: Association for Asian Studies and University of Hawaii Press, 2000).

14 Joanna Kidd, 'China's Naval Expansion', *Strategic Pointers*, 13 December 2000.

15 Khaild Mahmud, 'Rebuilding Sino-Indian Relations (1988–2000) – Rocky Path, Uncertain Destination', *Regional Studies*, vol. 19, no. 1, Winter 2000–2001, p. 19.

16 Peter Jensen, 'Chinese Sea Power and American Strategy', *Strategic Review*, Summer 2000, pp. 18–26.

17 Kidd, 'China's Naval Expansion'.

18 Reinhard Drifte, 'Japan's Energy Policy in Asia: Cooperation, Competition, Territorial Disputes', on www.cepmlp.org.

19 Fereidun Fesharaki, 'Energy and the Asian Security Nexus', *Journal of International Affairs*, vol. 53, no. 1, fall 1999, p. 92.

20 Alastair Iaian Johnston, 'China's Militarised Interstate Dispute Behaviour, 1949–1992: A First Cut at the Data', *China Quarterly*, no. 153, March 1998.

21 Evan A. Feigenbaum, 'China's Military Posture and the New Economic Geopolitics', *Survival*, vol. 41, no. 2, Summer 1999, pp. 71–88.

22 Lee Lai To, 'The South China Sea: China and Multilateral Dialogues', *Security Dialogue*, vol. 30, no. 2, June 1999, p. 166.

23 *Ibid*, p. 169.

24 The Shanghai Cooperation Organisation was previously called the Shanghai 5. For the background, see Gregory Gleason, 'Policy Dimensions of West Asian Borders after the Shanghai Accord', *Asian Perspective*, vol. 25, no. 1, 2001, pp. 107–31.

25 One Russian analyst has not injudiciously described the change in the economic balance of power as 'one of the most dramatic about-faces in the history of international economic relations' in Dmitri Trenin, *Russia's China Problem* (Washington, DC: Carnegie Endowment for International Peace, 1999), p. 4.

26 The concern that this generates in some circles in Russia can be seen in Alexander Pikayev, 'The Finlindization of Russia? The Kremlin's Geopolitical and Geo-economic Choices', *Program on New Approaches to Russian Security*, Policy memo no. 24, April 2000.

27 For a pessimistic assessment of this, see Stephen J. Blank, 'The Strategic Context of Russo-Chinese Relations', *Issues and Studies*, vol. 36, no. 4, July/August 2000, pp. 66–94.

28 John Calabrese, 'China's Policy Towards Central Asia: Renewal and Accommodation', *Eurasian Studies*, no. 16, Autumn–Winter 1999, p. 92.

29 David Lague and Trish Saywell, 'A Growing Storm for East Asia', *Far Eastern Economic Review*, 17 May 2001.

30 The prospect of a Russian withdrawal is explored in Martha Brill Olcott, 'Russian-Chinese Relations and Central Asia' in Shermann W. Garnett (ed.),

Rapprochement or Rivalry?: Russia-China Relations in a Changing World (Washington, DC: Carnegie Endowment for International Peace, 2000), pp. 371–402. See also Roland Dannreuther, 'Can Russia Sustain Its Dominance in Central Asia?', *Strategic Dialogue*, vol. 32, no. 2, June 2001, pp. 245–58.

31 For a Chinese assessment, see Li Jingjie, 'Pillars of the Sino-Russian Partnership', *Orbis*, Fall 2000, pp. 527–39.

32 See, for example, Jennifer Anderson, 'Limits of Sino-Russian Strategic Partnership', *Adelphi Paper 315* (Oxford: Oxford University Press for the IISS, 1997).

33 Similar conclusions can be found in Falah al-Jibury *et al.*, 'Cultural Security Perceptions in Northeast Asia and their Impact on Energy Cooperation', *Center for International Political Economy and the James Baker III Institute for Public Policy Working Paper*, May 2000. The potential for North Korea becoming an energy bridge is discussed in Kent E. Calder, 'The New Face of Northeast Asia', *Foreign Affairs*, vol. 80, no 1, January/February 2001, p. 107.

34 The various proposals are described in Mark J. Valencia and James P. Dorian, 'Mulitilateral Cooperation in Northeast Asia's Energy Sector: Possibilities and Problems', *Policy Paper 36*, University of California Institute on Global Conflict and Cooperation, 1998; and Paik, *Gas and Oil in Northeast Asia*, pp. 261–274.

35 'China's Congress Calls for National Oil Reserve', *Strafor.com*, 10 March 2000 in www.stratfor.com.

36 International Energy Agency, *China's Worldwide Quest for Energy Security* (Paris: OECD/IEA, 2000), pp. 48–9.

37 Philip Andrews-Speed, 'The Politics of Petroleum and the Energy Charter Treaty as an Effective Investment Regime', *Journal of Energy Finance and Development*, 1999.

38 'China Considers Participation in the work of the Energy Charter', *Alexander's Oil and Gas Connections: News and Trends: E & SE Asia*, vol. 6, no. 15, 14 August 2001.

39 Keun-Wook Paik and Jae-Yong Choi, 'Pipeline Gas in Northeast Asia: Recent Developments and Regional Perspectives', *Royal Institute of International Affairs*, January 1998.

40 Adrian J. Bradbrook, 'Electric Power Interconnection in North-East Asia: Towards a North-East Asian Energy Charter', unpublished report from the North-East Asia Expert Group Meeting on Inter-Country Cooperation in Electric Power Sector Development, 23–24 October 2001, Khabarovsk. Economic and Social Commission for Asia and the Pacific.

41 A good general discussion can be found in Aaron L. Friedberg, 'Will Europe's Past be Asia's Future?', *Survival*, vol. 42, no. 3 Autumn 2000, pp. 147–159.

42 Gerald M. Steinberg, 'Chinese Policies on Arms Control and Proliferation in the Middle East', *China Report*, vol. 34, no. 3–4, 1998, p. 382.

43 The energy analyst, Fereidun Fesharaki, notes that 'a mysterious trading company under the Chinese Defence Ministry – outside of the normal state oil-importing apparatus – imports 150,000-plus bpd from Iran'. See 'The Influence of Asia on Oil Price Fluctuations', *Alexander's Gas and Oil Connections: News and Trends: E and SE Asia*, vol. 6, no. 15, 14 August 2001.

44 Figures taken from US Congressional Research Service as quoted in Evan S. Medeiros and Bates Gill, *Chinese Arms Exports: Policy, Players and Process* (Carlisle, PA: Strategic Studies Institute, 2000), pp. 6–7. See also Daniel L. Byman and Roger Cliff, *China's Arms Sales: Motivations and Implications* (Santa Monica, CA: Rand, 1999).

45 Yitzhak Schichor, 'Mountains out of Molehills: Arms Transfers in the Sino-Middle Eastern Relations', *Middle East Review of International Affairs (MERIA)*, vol. 4, no. 3, September 2000.

46 This is extensively covered in Michael Eisenstadt, 'Russian Arms and Technology Transfers to Iran: Policy Challenges for the United States', *Arms Control Today*, March 2001, pp. 15–22. A significant event in November 2000 was the Russian abrogation of the Gore-Chernomyrdin agreement to restrict Russian conventional arms sales to Russia.

47 Bates Gill, 'Chinese Arms Exports to Iran', *Middle East Review of International Affairs*, vol. 2, no. 2, May 1998. Jing-dong Yuan, 'The Evolution of Chinese Non-Proliferation Policy, 1989–1999: Progress, Problems and Prospects', *International Studies Association Conference Paper*, 14–18 March 2000. Evan S. Medeiros, 'China, WMD Proliferation, and the "China Threat" Debate', *Issues*

and Studies, vol. 36, no. 1, January/February 2000.

48 Bates Gill and Evan S. Medeiros, 'Foreign and Domestic Influences on China's Arms Control and Non-proliferation Policies', *The China Quarterly*, 2000, p. 75.

49 Bates, 'Chinese Arms Exports to Iran', pp. 10–11.

50 Ralph A. Cossa, 'The Bush Presidency: Prospects for Sino-US Arms Control', *Disarmament Diplomacy*, December 2000/January 2001, p. 3.

51 This has been called by some Chinese analysts as the strategy of 'two imports and one export' as noted in Erica Strecker Downs, *China's Quest for Energy Security* (Santa Monica, CA: RAND, 2000), pp. 48–9.

52 Interview in Beijing, 30 November 2000.

53 See, for example, Yang Guang, 'China's Stabilising Role in the Middle East' in John Calabrese (ed.), *Gulf–Asia Enemy Security* (Washington, DC: Middle East Institute, 1998); and Xiaodong Zhang, 'China's Interest in the Middle East: Present and Future', *Middle East Policy*, vol. 4, no. 3, February 1999.

54 Medeiros, 'China, WMD Proliferation, and the "China Threat" Debate'.

55 Stephen Fidler and James Kynge, 'Stand-Off over Spyplane Escalates', *Financial Times*, 5 April 2001.